Hogbin on Woodturning

H
O

Hogbin on Woodturning

Masterful Projects Uniting Purpose, Form & Technique

Stephen Hogbin

Steeple Table. This simple table illustrates basic spindle-turning concepts that are also useful for making stools (page 130). The four legs were bundled together and turned as a single spindle, then separated. The conic connectors reinforce the rail-to-leg joints. The letters on the seat spell HOPE, resulting from an artistic collaboration discussed on page 130.
Photo by Michael McLuhan.

Fox Chapel Publishing

ISBN 978-1-56523-752-0

Library of Congress Cataloging-in-Publication Data

Hogbin, Stephen.
Hogbin on woodturning / Stephen Hogbin.
pages cm
Includes index.
Summary: "Legendary woodturner Stephen Hogbin's work has been groundbreaking at every turn. He first burst on the scene in the early 1970s with an exhibition of turnings like no one had ever seen--cut apart, re-assembled, enhanced by carving, and bearing little resemblance to the standard round stuff that characterized the lathe. Now the internationally recognized designer examines ten of his finest and most innovative creations, and distills each piece to a useful project that any woodturner can replicate. This is the first time that Hogbin has described his techniques and presented his ideas in step-by-step project format. All of these projects begin with the lathe, but each features inventive cutting into the turned elements and recombining the pieces to make entirely new forms. They do not require advanced technical skills, but will encourage you to break out of the basic vocabulary of woodturning and see its marvelous new possibilities. Hogbin on Woodturning reveals how a master designer integrates his visionary concepts with practical work at the lathe, allowing each to feed into the other. By replicating Hogbin's turning methods in your own home workshop, you'll gain stimulating new insight into the lathe and discover how to get the most out of your craft"-- Provided by publisher.
ISBN 978-1-56523-752-0 (pbk.)
1. Turning (Lathe work) I. Title.
TT201.H615 2013
736'.4--dc23
2012028947

To learn more about the other great books from Fox Chapel Publishing, or to find a retailer near you, call toll-free 800-457-9112 or visit us at *www.FoxChapelPublishing.com*.

Note to Authors: We are always looking for talented authors to write new books. Please send a brief letter describing your idea to Acquisition Editor, 1970 Broad Street, East Petersburg, PA 17520.

Printed in China
First printing

Acknowledgements

Thanks to Mark Sfirri for suggesting many times that another book would be helpful and interesting after *Wood Turning: the Purpose of the Object*. There was also a conversation through emails about the ideas and possible content amongst a group of woodturners that included Mark, Stan Wellborn, Gary Guenther, and David Fry. Thank you to The Ginger Press publisher and bookshop owner Maryann Thomas for her suggestions and guidance for all things book. Simon Kitz and Tom Jenks worked with me over the time this book was being written. Their discussions at break time, and their review of some chapters, was invaluable—along with their impeccable workmanship on some of the projects. Margaret Ballantyne, my partner, has a sharp eye and critical approach to all things visual and colorful. Michael McLuhan photographed the finished works. The Bruce County Museum has organized the first public exhibition of the work from the book. Most of all, thanks to the exceptional editor and good friend John Kelsey.

Thanks to the great many students who have taken my classes and workshops, represented by this group portrait of my class at Anderson Ranch, Colorado, in the summer of 2008. I've learned something from most of you, and hope that you have learned something from me too.

On large projects I am both team leader and crew member, collaborating closely with clients, architects, helpers, and tradesmen. My installation crew for the Toronto library screen, 1976, included from left to right my in-laws Michael Thomas and Bud Thomas, plus the furniture maker Stephen Harris, a great asset on site, highly capable and unflappable.

Dedication

To my brothers Geoff, Brian, and Peter, for their support and encouragement over three score years and ten, from childhood to middle age.

Contents

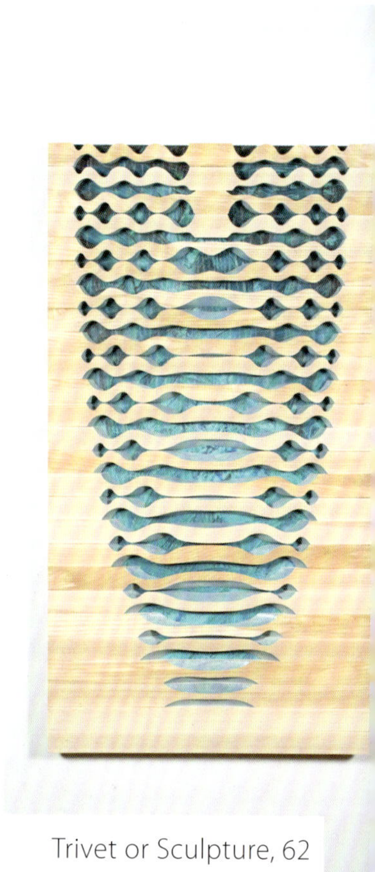

The Walking Bowl, 92

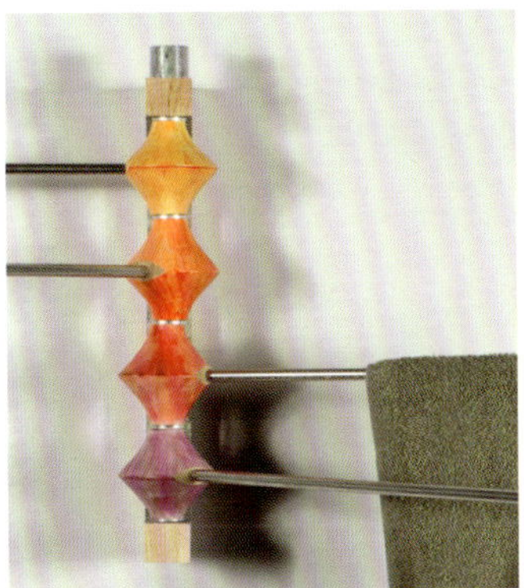
Towel Rack, 72

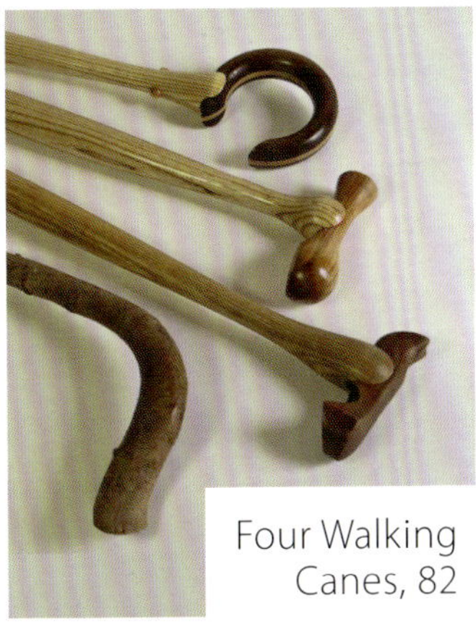
Four Walking Canes, 82

Stool Collaboration, 130

Batch of Boxes, 110

Steeple Table, 122

What you can learn from this book

The projects in this book reflect on old and new work. The order is not chronological, but rather a way to tell the story via the making of the object. Each project is presented in a step-by-step format, with sidebar discussions of important concepts and galleries of related objects.

These forms have been called "fragmentals." Everything is a fragment of something else. The project you make comes from a board and the board comes from a tree and the tree from a forest. A piece of wood can be turned, cut into fragments, then joined back together in a new configuration.

Fragments reveal the magic of the cross section

Spindle turnings cut in half become salad servers, candleholders, trays (Chapters 1, 2 3).

Spindle turnings cut in quarters become legs for tables, stools, and chairs (Chapters 2, 11, 12).

Faceplate turnings cut apart become unusual bowls, boxes, and flowing sculptures (Chapters 4, 5, 6, 9, 10).

The lathe can make parts for larger projects, such as canes, towel racks, handles, and many other household objects (Chapters 5, 7, 8).

You'll learn how to…

… turn green wood (Chapters 2, 3)

… build blanks from boards (Chapter 4)

… turn thick planks (Chapter 9)

… turn difficult wood (Chapters 5, 9)

… apply color (Chapters 3, 4, 6, 7, 9, 10)

…and explore ideas (throughout the book).

Foreword

About Stephen Hogbin

BY MARK SFIRRI

Imagine that you're several years into your woodworking career and you have the brilliant idea to turn a piece of wood that's 77" in diameter by 14" thick, over 450 board feet of Western red cedar. Then imagine actually doing it! And doing it almost forty years ago, when variable speed woodturning lathes were in their infancy and hardly sufficient. But that's what Stephen Hogbin did, and while this accomplishment doesn't begin to define him, his feat of engineering and personal bravery still resonate. He cut the huge disk into pieces and created two chairs, a table, and a shelf, a concept that he had worked out in miniature (photo below). This work was the centerpiece for the 1974 exhibition in Toronto that gained him international recognition.

Hogbin was born in England in 1942. In the late 1950s he studied woodworking at Rycotewood College and then industrial design at the Royal College of Art. One of his professors there was David Pye, an important maker who wrote the seminal books, *The Nature and Art of Workmanship* and *The Nature and Aesthetics of Design*. Hogbin was impressed with Pye's design insight, that "he engaged the whole mind in looking at workmanship, objects, and quality." In 1968 Hogbin moved to Canada to teach at Sheridan College School of Design, where he taught full-time until 1972. He later settled in Lake Charles, about three hours north. He lives and works there still.

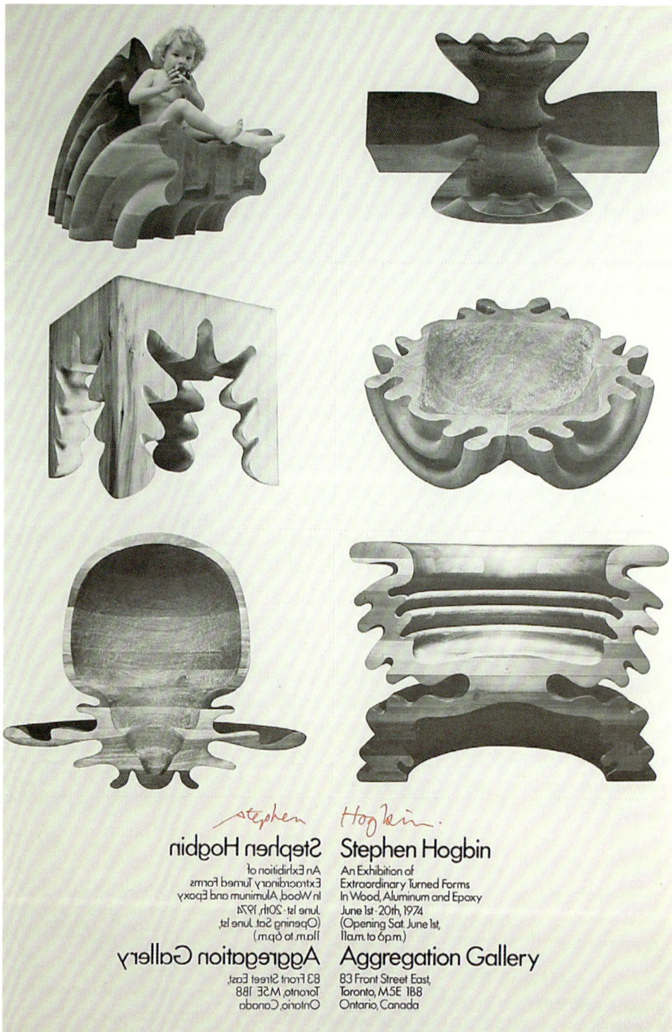

1974 poster. Hogbin's Aggregation Gallery exhibition won international attention.

Big disk. One large turning generated a suite of furniture.

Beyond utility

Until 1970, woodturning was nearly exclusively devoted to utilitarian objects. Bob Stocksdale's bowls were the first to elevate the work through his high level of craftsmanship, careful wood selection, and attention to detail. But in the early 1970s, Hogbin was developing vessels in a different way. He turned some honeycombed wood and saw several options: throw the bowl away, fill in the blemish, or remove the defect. He decided to cut the bowl in half. He looked at the cross section and considered different ways of recombining the pieces, beginning a series of explorations into cut and reassembled pieces that he called "fragmentals" (page 68).

If you are designing an object in advance of turning it, you need to draw the cross section, but you usually never see it in the finished work. In most vessels, the line of the interior and exterior are parallel, maintaining uniform wall thickness. Hogbin intentionally made the interior and exterior contours different to create graphic effects via the revealed cross section. Space for a Bowl, made in 1972 and shown on page 11, is a good example. He turned a bowl form, cut it in half, and glued it together along what had been its top rim, creating a form similar to a half walnut.

Hogbin next turned his attention to the question of scale. "The size of the turnings was being determined by the size of a board, which was limiting, and gluing two boards together always looked to me like I couldn't find a board big enough. But many boards might be different. Then the questions: how big might a piece be? What is the best and proper scale to be working at? Some of my forms would work as a button and also, if scaled up, become big enough to be a large sculpture on a wall. All I needed was a lathe big enough."

Bud Thomas, his then father-in-law, suggested using a truck axle and differential as the mechanism for a homemade variable speed lathe, which would provide the slowness necessary to turn large forms. House jacks wedged the bed between floor and ceiling, to keep the lathe from dancing all over the place (drawing on page 12).

As a result of his ground-breaking exhibition in 1974, Hogbin was offered a residency at Melbourne State College. In 1980 he published a book chronicling his experience, *Wood Turning: The Purpose of the Object*. It didn't follow the "how-to" approach, common then and now, but was based on concept and design. The heart of the book, however, is the gallery section showing the objects produced during his residency: "bowl investigations" (pages 50 and 107), furniture (pages 33, 122, and 130), and an assortment of other functional pieces including racks (page 72), spoons (page 31), scoops, whisks, bookends, and a series of salad servers. This remarkable collection of work provided the inspiration for this new book, *Hogbin on Woodturning*.

The most remarkable object in that first book is the "Egg Cup." I remember the first time I saw the image reproduced at right. I froze. While it clearly contained turned elements, it transcended easy understanding. To this day, it remains my favorite turned object. It was made by working from a block of wood about 8 in (204mm) square by about 1 in (25mm) thick, turning only the two faces. It was then cut into four pieces and glued face-to-face and edge-to-edge. It seemed to me to be twenty years ahead of its time. Now, nearly forty years later, it is still twenty years ahead of its time.

A new chapter in Hogbin's career opened in the mid-1970s as a result of a faceplate turning that he sliced into strips, rotating each strip 90° to create a small screen. An architect approached him about making something similar on a larger scale. Hogbin was game, even when he realized that the plan called for a wall over 200 feet long and 7 feet tall! Undeterred, he once again invented a machine to make it possible, which he called a variable-arm milling machine (page 12 and 117). He thought that by moving the tool instead of the wood, he could expand the size of the object that he could produce. He says, "I see my work as developing a vocabulary of techniques, forms, and ideas that may be returned to, and that will set up thinking about a new idea. Exploring turning was too single technique focused, but the milling machine had the same potential. So I did both while trying to sort out what the content was about."

Half walnut. Hogbin began to cut and reassemble bowls with experimental pieces like this, titled Space for a Bowl and made in 1972.

Egg Cup. This startling object was made in 1975 from a single square of wood, turned on both sides, then cut and reassembled.

In the early 1980s, Hogbin revisited the vessel form in his "Walking Bowl" series (page 92). Unlike the earlier experiments, this work abandons symmetry. The form is turned with long flanges, and then cut in half. The top edge is glued together, but the halves are shifted so that it is no longer symmetrical and the flanges elevate the bowl form. As sculptor and collector Robyn Horn observes, "Stephen's work is far-reaching. His concept of reworking the turned piece, of cutting segments apart and reassembling them, started many of us looking at the lathe in a different way. Rather than limiting process, the lathe could be used as an avenue toward sculpture."

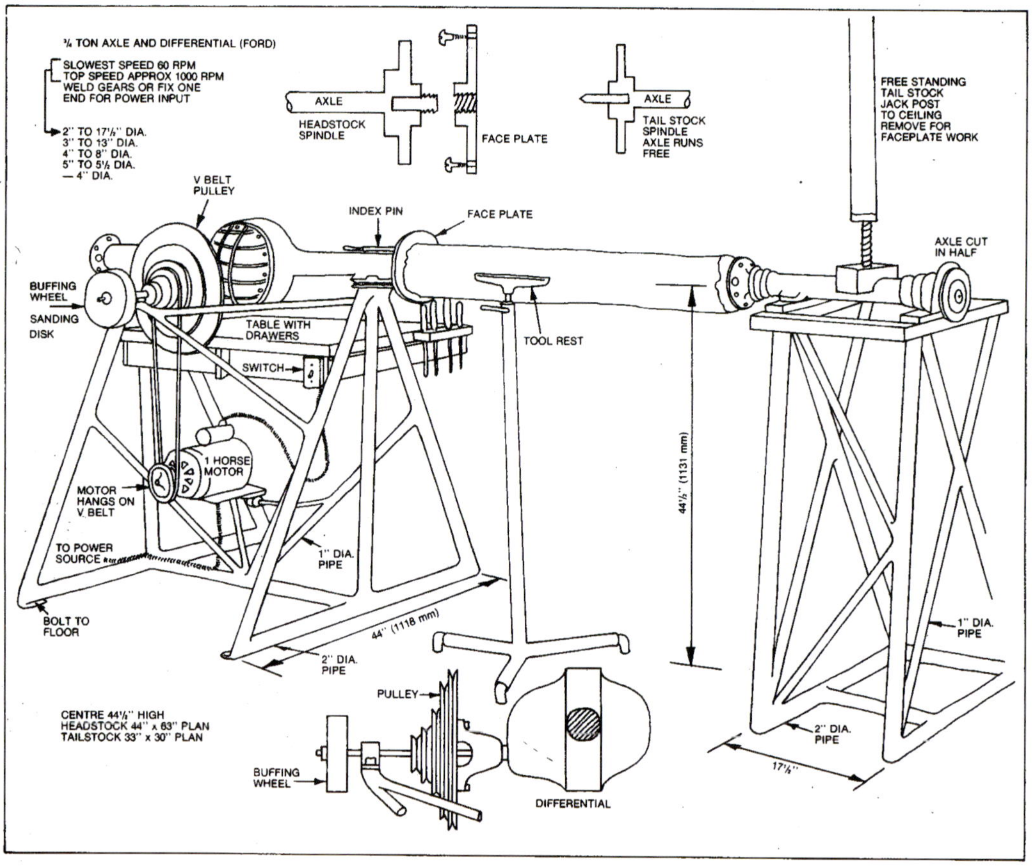

Truck axle. Hogbin's first big lathe could swing a 7-foot disk.

Milling machine. The variable-arm milling machine features a router motor mounted on an arm that pivots from a central mast. It solves the problem of "turning" very large forms.

New Directions

But Hogbin's direction was about to change yet again, as he explains: "In the early eighties I resolved to back away from the turning field. Many wonderful people, highly skilled and imaginative, were taking the domain forward…It also felt too competitive and that is not a good environment for me to work in." Hogbin now had a desire to act locally and regionally with an eye toward conservation. He branched out to collaborate on designs for outdoor public spaces. This work is particularly satisfying for him because many more people can experience the finished product. The public installations, beginning with the 200 foot library wall, made him well known in the region, introducing him to a clientele for custom residential work. These projects combine built-in and free-standing furniture, cabinetry, and staircases (photo at right).

In 2000 Hogbin published his second book, *Appearance & Reality: A Visual Handbook for Artists, Designers and Makers*, written as a resource for designing in general and expanding on the ideas and categories in his first book. In 2010 he published a third book, *Evaluating: The Critique in the Studio Workshop*. Both are available from The Ginger Press in Owen Sound, Ontario, www.gingerpress.com. In 2007, Hogbin (along with Giles Gilson and Mark Lindquist) was an inaugural recipient of the American Association of Woodturners' Professional Outreach Program Merit Award for his lifetime achievements and the influence he's had on contemporary woodturning.

Library wall. Commissioned in 1976 for the central library in downtown Toronto, this undulating wall was made using the variable arm milling machine.

Hogbin on Woodturning, this fourth book, further reveals the depth of thought that goes into the objects that Hogbin makes. He says, "Perhaps others see my activity as nothing more than a utilitarian product, whereas I see what I make as a set of human values with a story. The object is the outcome, the physical manifestation, of the story, or as I prefer, the song."

After forty years, Hogbin's work is still completely on the cutting edge. I asked him if he would make the large Western red cedar chairs again and he gave the answer that I expected, which was no. The reason, however, was a surprise. I assumed that physical self-preservation stopped him, because it's such a dangerous undertaking. But his concern now is conservation: he could build six chairs with the wood he used to make one. He assured me that he had no fear of the physical risk at all. Perhaps this same fearlessness has allowed him to thrive as a creative designer and maker for all of these years, never letting what seem to be insurmountable obstacles get in his way.

Staircase. Hogbin's recent work includes a number of complex furniture and staircase installations.

Mark Sfirri is a woodworker and turner who lives in New Hope, Pennsylvania. He is the coordinator and professor in the Fine Woodworking Program at Bucks County Community College in Newtown, Pennsylvania. In 2009 Sfirri won the Washington, DC, James Renwick Alliance distinguished educator award, and in 2012 he received the Lifetime Achievement Award from the Collectors of Wood Art. An earlier version of this essay appeared in Woodwork magazine, February 2008.

Introduction

Today at 6:30 a.m., the sun shines orange through the window onto a print of the landscape. Today there are several projects with which to engage. But first I shower, dress, walk the dog, breakfast, and lace up the old soft work boots.

A quick look at emails but I must be careful not to get distracted. The studio is still dark but inviting. Freshly cut wood scents the air. The light illuminates the settled dust from yesterday's flurry of activity, projects where we left off, various parts at different stages of making. The morning tea raises awareness along with the pleasure of sorting out the procedures. One step at a time, nothing missed, but no unnecessary steps either. The balance that guides this maker's life lies in the working experience amongst searching for quality, finding economies, and just having fun.

Today there are parts to be turned, cut up, then glued together for the table (page 122). On the bench close to the lathe are the four blanks milled, finished on the inside and strapped together with a smidgen of glue at the ends. It's 7:30, another hour before my assistant arrives. If I get the turning done and then hand off the pieces we will glue the four legs to the table frame. My attention can move on to the wall-hung sculpture (page 62).

The drawings are clear, the details worked out, and yet the final resolution will be on the lathe. Going from the flat surface to the round is always a challenge. I love to draw with a soft pencil on crisp white paper in quiet reverie, leaning over the drawing board as the lines connect, intersect, curl around, and bring coherence to the imagined forms. What I saw in the mind's eye and what happens on paper are always challenging to bring together. The piece grows in the flow among the essentially different activities of thinking, drawing, and making.

Flow

This thing of flow is difficult to get right. The unconscious has a way of presenting its best idea unexpectedly. The cross section is determined in the drawing but the materials may have more to say. If I listen, observe, and play the tools attentively, today's version will be better than the last time. My practice is the craft of materials and, at the moment, the craft of writing, but most important, the craft of the imagination. Even though I have made something like this before, this is the first time for this piece, never before has it lived, and how long will it last? Longer than me and certainly longer than today.

I turn the legs first with a roughing-out gouge and then take the finest cut with a small sharp gouge, no fibers ripped. A freshly sharpened scraper removes tiny ribs and refines the lines. I pull the turning from the lathe, stand it on end and assess it, consult the drawing, compare with another recent piece. The form needs thinning, so back to the lathe. Eventually a light sanding, and finally away from the lathe I saw the ends square on the chop-saw to eliminate the glue, then shape the top of the leg using bastard and mill files.

Morning banter begins with the assistant and then breaks away to the job at hand. "Let's run a checklist for this glue up. The parts are on the bench. This is the way it will go. We need bar and band clamps, blocks to protect the leg, glue and brush, dry cloth to wipe hands and a damp cloth for spills, framing square and tape measure," and on the list goes with everything in easy reach. I am a stickler for the right amount of glue and the joint must be full so no air can get in but only a tiny bead emerges, a pearl necklace. Each assistant brings skills and today we are taping around the joint to resist the glue, rather than the wax-release method. Either method reduces cleanup time.

Quiet space. Hogbin's work table gets plenty of natural light. He prefers to work in silence, without the distractions of music or conversation, but with regular breaks for convivial tea.

Turning tools. Nothing fancy here. Gouges for roughing out, scrapers for smoothing cuts, parting tool or bedan for fillets and small details.

Mentoring

I have my own ways of doing things but I also see making as a social activity and I don't have much interest in the master-pupil relationship. Mentoring is a gentler way of connecting, of being present and not overbearing. Mind and hands need to live in a community. Who am I working with, who is the client, how will this project impact on the environment—conversations for tea break. The military when marching take a brief break every hour, and that way they can march all day. Working has a rhythm and too much stress on the mind or body is unhealthy, even dangerous. In my shop tea and cookies are mandatory at regular intervals; in the long run these breaks support efficiency.

Back in the workshop the leather-hard glue needs to be removed from the table; then it's time to finish sanding with ever-finer abrasives. I go to the lathe. The false faceplate holds the strips for the sculpture. The turning is easy and the resulting form will be lively and dramatic—that is, if I get this part right. I consult the sketchbook and think about the concept of flow, then feel it through my hands as I work on the wood. It is as much an emotion as a conceptual target, a subjective feeling as a measurable objective. The piece is about my experience, the subject of flow, an object to behold, and a context in which it will fit. My freshly sharpened scraping chisel will balance these elements. The angle of the ground chisel is much less interesting than the shape to be turned, though harmony between the two is essential.

I quickly rough out the first part of the turning. Adjusting the light next to the lathe shows the strength of highlights and shadows. A good sculpture must survive in poor lighting as well as in the perfect environment of the gallery. Where will the piece spend most of its life? When I add color, how will the light reveal the form? The chisel gets sharpened again for the final pass, leaving a finish close to what I want. It'll only need a light sanding.

Fragments. Cutting into the faceplate turning reveals its cross section. Paint emphasizes the flowing lines.

Split spindles. Cutting into the spindle turning produces two or more slender elements suitable for handles, cross-rails, or table legs.

Mistakes

Mistakes happen almost every day and what counts is the ability to work with the situation. It's very rare that we need to remake something. Twice over the decades of making, drawers came out the wrong size. I always tell a new assistant it's okay to make mistakes, I make them all the time; what is important is how do you turn the mistake to your advantage. Recently someone said they had no idea I made mistakes because the finished work always looks so perfect. Flattering indeed, but the reality is, if you are not making mistakes your skills are not being tested or extended. Trying not to make the same mistake again teaches a broad understanding of the issues involved.

My assistant jolts the reverie of making with a question about how to finish a detail. To what level should we take this work? We briefly discuss the relationship between economics and design. This design fits the client's budget, and then we finish the work to our usual standard. The studio workshop is silent except for the sound of the tool; sometimes the loon on the lake makes a call, and there's the occasional grunt of satisfaction. I find music and conversation distracting. When working on site the radios of the tradesmen make it very difficult to concentrate. My work is not boring and every project is new for me, so it needs concentration to feel the sensuality of the materials and leave the mind free to resolve the problems.

Mentoring. Hogbin and a recent assistant, Simon Kitz, test the strength of a boardroom table. Working collaboratively adds a social dimension to the process of designing and making. The complete table is shown below.

I apply undercoat paint to the finished turning while it's on the lathe and then leave it to dry over lunch while we have another go-round on the issues of economics and aesthetics, workmanship of risk, workmanship of certainty. We discuss the bodgers who worked in the forests making Windsor chairs, the structures and finish they achieved. Compare that to the work of the urban makers who turned for William Morris—how was that work finished? The sculptors Barbara Hepworth or Henry Moore each worked toward different surfaces appropriate to their own aesthetic.

The conversation comes back to the shop and my equipment. I explain why there are three lathes. The first belonged to the late furniture maker Stephen Harris, which I used when sharing a workshop with him. I still have it as a nostalgic object and a memory of him. The next lathe was made from a truck axle in 1973. Scale was the issue rather than finish, but inevitably this large lathe could not achieve a good furniture finish, though it continues to be useful for sculpture. The lathe I mostly use today, which you'll see in photos throughout this book, is a standard machine with a 16-inch swing, typical of many workshops. For larger works I would probably move to the milling machine (page 117).

No Rushing, No Dawdling

Lunch is over and I quickly check emails, then go back to work. The finish goes on today, but it is the first coat, and in total there are three for the color and then three for the clear finish. Nothing good comes from rushing; speed is a killer of projects and of people for that matter. I prefer to stick with a no-growth economy with exceptional quality in the finished product. Good for the environment, good for the future. I live on an island of meaning in a sea of consumerism.

The sculpture is for the reception room in a corporate office. The office colors are specific and not too subtle. The sculpture will bring depth and variety to the space, unifying materials and existing forms. Conceptually it looks at chaos theory and fractals, much to the surprise of the client who chuckled at the idea of chaos in his offices. With most of my clients I find a wonderful rapport as we discover common threads to explore. Later today the client will visit to look at progress.

I take the sculpture from the lathe and separate the parts while maintaining their order. I want to look at alternate configurations and will shuffle these parts like a deck of cards (page 66). I'll photograph each design that emerges—it's impossible to remember all the variations and I may make new discoveries.

Now I choose and mix colors in an old paper coffee cup. Applied with a fine brush, the paint has dried on the first pieces by the time I get to the end. A wash will knock back the brightness, specks of the first color show through, giving the finish a lively active look. It's ready to show the client the direction of the work.

Progress

The table moves along well and my assistant is wiping on its first coat of urethane. Meanwhile I am staging the space for the client's visit. The website presents a great variety of projects, but the image of a piece is no substitute for physical reality and the alchemy of making. In our image-besotted culture, people who don't work with their hands get a special charge from the sensuality of making. Makers need to share the magic and this means being ready to apply the second coat on the table when the client walks in. The theatre of making isn't my best side, but makers who do master the theatrics will enthuse their clients. The client needs to be handed experiences that make good dinner-party stories.

Back to the sculpture: I lay out the parts in an order relating to the concept of the piece. Ideas of flow, water reflection, and slats of wood all suggest the water's edge. The undercoat now gets its sky-blue first coat of acrylic paint. It almost works but it's not reflective enough. Interference paint adds some shine and on it goes until I can feel the depths of Georgian Bay's blue waters (page 66).

Later in the afternoon the client circles through and spends more time than anybody intended. He makes the usual exclamations about the big band saw, an old patternmaker's cast-iron machine that impresses anyone with a technical bent. Every client has to be educated about the thinking and processes we use in the workshop, and in return the conversation will become rich with understanding of one another's needs. When we achieve a symbiosis the work seems to keep flowing with new projects over the years. The actual making itself is about half of what needs to be understood to engage with the client.

Before evening I will look further into Bob Weile's book *One Smart World* and refresh my thinking around creativity, understanding, decision-making and personal spirit. The technologies of the mind need sharpening just as much as my pencil, plane, and shop processes.

Yes, I do enjoy woodturning, but most of all I enjoy the mix of ideas, form giving, making, and engaging with others. It's a whole process that is endlessly fascinating. By the end of today I will be looking forward to tomorrow.

—Stephen Hogbin, June 2012

CHAPTER 1

Spindle turning, cut and rejoined

Candleholder

Small gift kicks off design process

Some time ago the Philadelphia furniture maker Jack Larimore visited here with his family. It was a memorable visit on several counts, the most dramatic being a violent thunderstorm at three in the morning. They were to leave for the first ferry and had to be up and away during the storm. Later in the morning when I got up and went into the living room, Jack had left a wonderful candleholder on the table as a thank-you gift. It is a treasured object full of memories. It also got me thinking about what I would make for a candleholder. The design that follows is the result of that experience with the night, lightning, balance, and the sense of a precarious existence, human warmth, and friendship. Also, whenever I think about things in balance, the designs of Mark Sfirri (Design Influences below) and his stunning off-center turnings come to mind.

Design Influences

Some designs look oh so familiar. Where did I see it before? Am I copying or being inspired by others? I am struck how much my candleholders look like turnings by the Pennsylvania woodturner Mark Sfirri; it is a how-to Sfirri, with cut-and-glue by Hogbin.

Jack Larimore left his wonderful candleholder and Mark Sfirri had made inspirational off-center forms. I can connect these experiences quite clearly, and perhaps there are others, such as the brass candleholder that was passed on to me from a wonderful aunt. So much of what we make is caught up in memories of others and events. These associations bring depth and meaning to the commonplace and I think that is worth copying, because these moments resonate emotionally. Making connections is the basis for making good art. Sometimes it's for oneself and no one else gets the reference and that's okay. The magic starts when the work carries commonality, connection; it links our worlds together.

The Gift. The gift of a candleholder, made by the Philadelphia furniture artist Jack Larimore, kicked off the design process for this project.

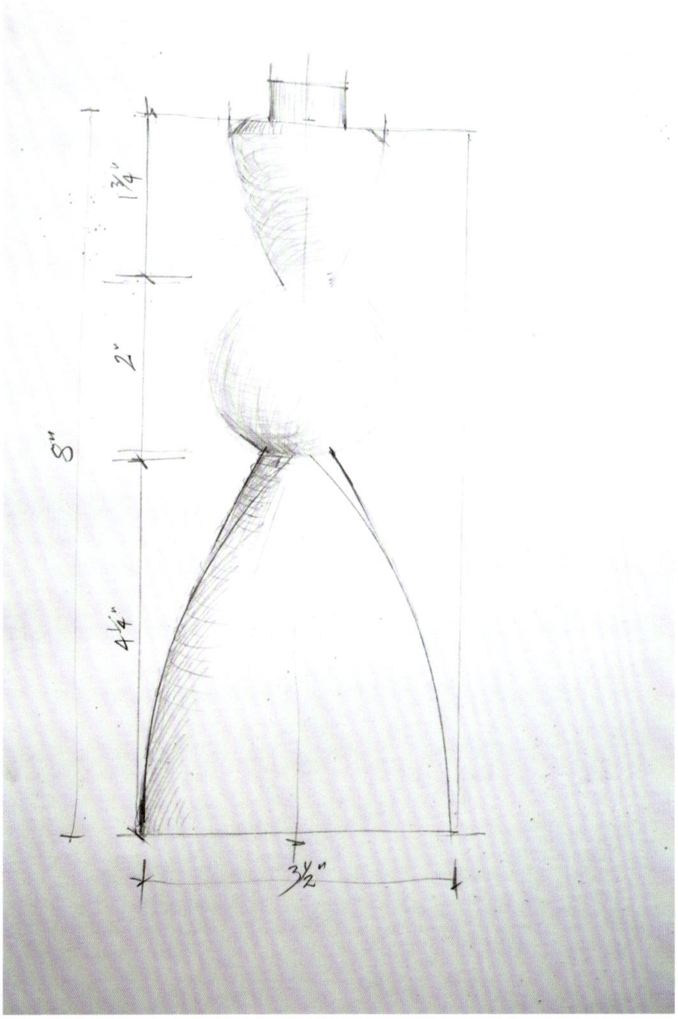

Drawing for candleholder.

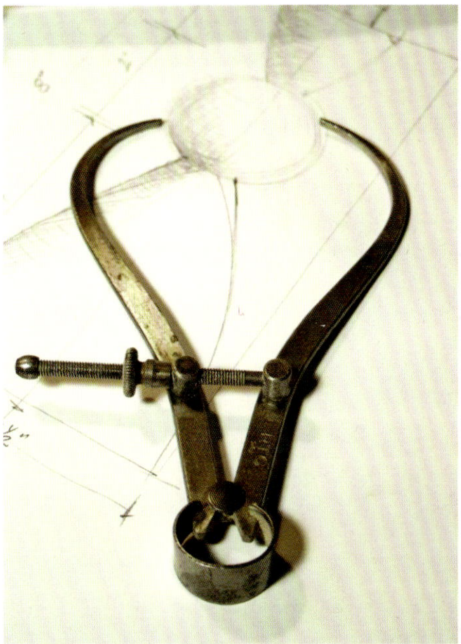

Dimensions. Use calipers to take dimensions directly from the drawing to the lathe.

PHOTO BY MICHAEL MCLUHAN

Candleholder, 2012. Maple, paint, copper ferrule, 12" (305mm) tall.

Turning the blank

1 **Wood.** The wood for this candleholder came from a maple walking-bowl off-cut 3½" (89mm) thick. This block was passed though the table saw for straight and clean cuts, then finished on the band saw.

2 **Turning blank.** While the block is square, mark out the diagonals and find the centers. Saw off the corners to form an octagonal blank.

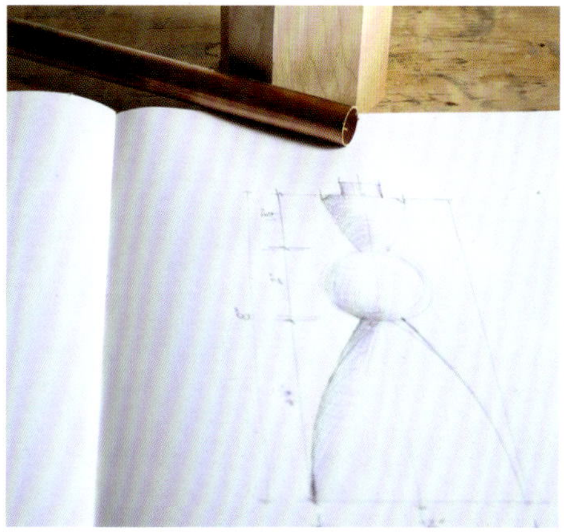

3 **Proportions.** The block determines the proportions of the piece. Usually I prefer to work the other way around, but this is a luxury depending on the wood you can get. This block is somewhat squat. I always make a drawing to work out the proportions and division of the shapes.

4 **Roughing.** Use a large gouge to round the blank to a cylinder and begin to establish the overall shape.

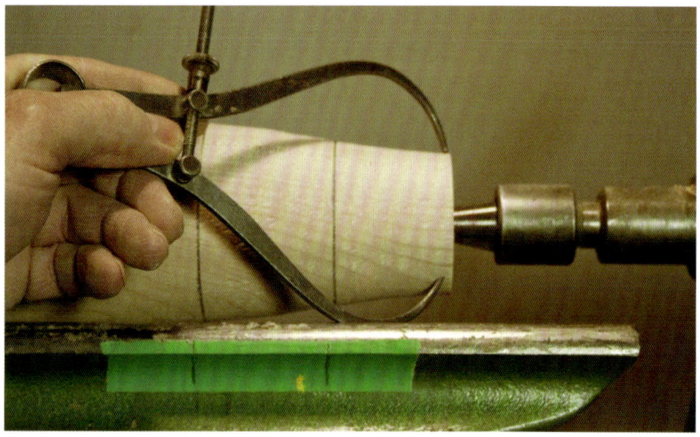

5 **Dimensions.** With the block of wood on the lathe and turned into a cylinder, you can begin to transfer the dimensions from the drawing.

6 **Smooth.** The round-nose scraper cleans up the rough turning and refines the forms.

7 **Detail.** The pointed scraper helps make small, sharp details.

Ferrule for fire safety

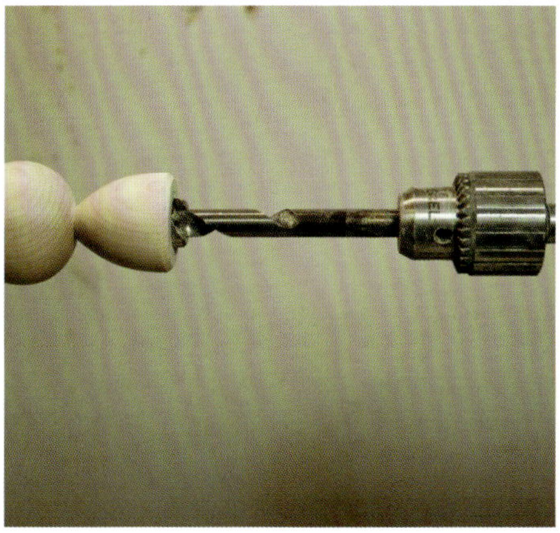

“If you don’t use a metal ferrule you can expect the candleholder to burn.”

8 **Ferrule.** Drill out the top of the candleholder on the lathe. It can be done on a drill press, but it’s always wobbly and not as satisfactory. The drill bit shown is a ⅞" (22mm) Forstner, the same size as the copper ferrule. If you don’t use a metal ferrule you can expect the candleholder to burn.

9 **Safety.** The charred wood in the photo is mild compared to what can and does happen after a party with people going to bed and finding in the morning the candleholder destroyed. Perhaps that is better than burning the house down.

Cutting and reconnecting

10 **Sawing.** I decided to cut the sphere at the center on a diagonal. Firm support is essential when band-sawing a round workpiece, to prevent it from rolling when the blade engages the wood. You could instead make the cut with a handsaw while holding the workpiece in the vise.

11 **Smoothing.** The cut needs to be sanded smooth and flat. The big sanding disk is invaluable; sheet sandpaper glued down on a board works as well, though not as quickly.

12 **Align.** Now the difficult choice about the reconnecting: how high, off-center or straight up should it be? I decided to pull the top up higher than previous pieces in the series. Mark with a pencil three points to help with alignment after you apply the glue.

13 **Evaluation.** Comparing to what's gone before is invaluable and it's possible to see that this one has more lift. It is a little chunky perhaps, even quirky, and what it lacks in height it has in character. While objects don't actually speak to us we often do project human qualities onto them.

14 **Rub joint.** With the uncut copper tubing in the hole at the top, the square helps align and glue the sphere together so the candle will sit up straight. This connection was not clamped but relied on a rub joint. Put on enough glue to get a tiny bead of squeeze-out.

Finishing

15 **Color.** The wood is a yellow brown and I am going for a complementary color. Directly opposite on the color wheel (page 41) is a blue-red. On the pot of paint it is called "ultramarine blue." It makes for a high contrast. I think of them as fairground colors, not so subtle but playful and lively.

16 **Varnish.** The final finish is a spray can of semi-gloss urethane varnish. Stand the workpiece upside down and spray the bottom first. Allow to fully dry, turn over, and do the top side.

From Drawing to Lathe: Design is a Compromise

The drawing is not the finished piece. It is a place to start, though the actual thing you are making soon takes over. Calipers help size things from the drawing. "Help" is the operative word — you have to pay attention to what is happening in the three-dimensional object as you go from a flat place to a round place.

When the turning is almost finished, I like to stop and take a careful look at the design by comparing it to earlier work. It looks a bit dumpy and sags into the ground. A little more turning and it gets lighter and more buoyant. Turnings by Rude Osolnik illustrate this rather well. These are the most elegant of forms but do have the potential of tipping over. The design worked on here is shorter and has a large footprint, less elegant perhaps but less likely to fall over. Everything is a compromise and choosing the best alternative is the challenge. What makes one thing better than another? Is it form, function, idea, or the balance within the object? Tough choices!

Proportions. The turned blank looks dumpy beside two previous candleholders.

Candleholder and Cup

A wonderful food

Chocolate, when beautifully made, is a wonderful food. How to present its specialness? The association seemed inevitable with the candleholders I was producing at this time. However, this piece was the first to be cut on the diagonal, which introduced a cubist look to the form. Without the cuts it looked ordinary. The cuts articulated the form, making it lively. Also, the clear demarcation between cup and stem perhaps makes the contents of the bowl even more precious.

Stopping for a snack

On a road trip with my partner Margaret and her daughter Walker, we stopped for a snack. Margaret and I munched on a box of six donuts with a fair bit of criticism from Walker. The box never quite got cleaned up and the following Christmas I made a wood donut, put it in the original box, and set it under the tree. Much hilarity ensued upon opening. The box came out at birthdays and Christmas with different donuts, and one was the donut tower. Its original title was Canadian Icon: Tedious Donuts Series, 2006. I still have the original box.

COLLECTION: IRVING LIPTON, YALE UNIVERSITY ART GALLERY PERMANENT COLLECTION.

Chocolate Cup, 1998. Walnut and paint, 12" (305mm) x 5½" (140mm).

COLLECTION: WALKER BALLANTYNE-HILL.

Walker's Donut Tower, 2006. Ash, paint; 13" (330mm) x 4" (102mm) dia.

CHAPTER 2

Spindle turning, cut and carved

Salad Servers

Wood from living with the wild

The porcupines developed a taste for fruit trees in the winter of 2011, as well as for the wiring under my van. I used every trick I knew without killing them. Then, as revealed after the spring snowmelt, many trees also had been ringed at their base by mice. It's tough being a tree with no means of escape. At least I could get the van into the garage. The wild pear trees took the worst gnawing and one was stripped almost top to bottom. So, we cut down this thirty-year-old tree and turned it into salad servers. Pear is a wonderful turning wood! The servers are an excellent project for introducing the fundamental concept in my work and in this book of turning a piece—in the instance a simple spindle—and cutting it in half to expose the cross section.

I work with three basic shapes. The servers illustrated in the photo sequence are fundamental and analogous to homemade bread. The other designs are, well, more designerly (see Turnings for Sale, page 31). These spoons are non-standard, individually made in response to the character of the wood. Each pair of spoons comes out a little different from the wild.

These servers are a production item for me, and over the years I have made many in different woods and sizes. Some were made by my assistants, most notably Amanda Wall-Graff. The servers shown here are two halves cut from a turning, and it's also possible to put four pieces together to make four spoons from one turning using the table-leg technique shown on pages 124-125. They also are an excellent gift item and this time a gift from the porcupine.

Simon Kitz joined me in the studio workshop for this photo sequence. A recent graduate of the furniture design program at Sheridan College in Oakville, Ontario, he was looking for a work experience with a chance to make his own projects on the side.

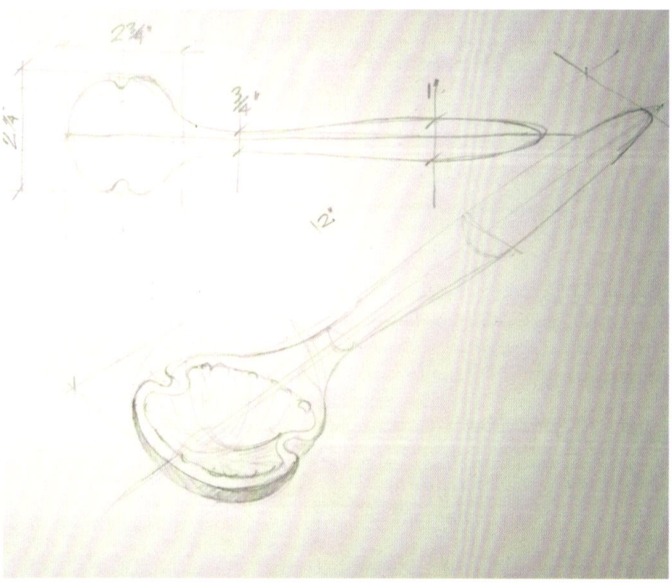

Two for one. A pair of serving spoons comes from a single turning band-sawn in half and carved. This is a quick project that establishes some of the fundamental ideas behind my work: cut into the turning, look for new ways to recombine and reuse the fragments.

"The fundamental concept in my work is turning a piece and then cutting it in half to expose the cross section."

Gift from the porcupines. This 30-year-old pear tree, gnawed to death by porcupines, yielded good turning wood for many pairs of spoons.

Turning and sawing

1 **Safety.** Simon bucks the wild pear log into turning billets. Simon had not used a chain saw before but here is working safely with boots, helmet with ear and eye protection, and Kevlar chaps. The buck stabilizes the log; Simon stands to the side of the cut, clear of kickback.

2 **Cylinders.** We turned ten billets to basic cylinders for making into spoons, some to be turned green immediately, and some left to dry with their ends sealed by some old PVA glue.

3 **Green fun.** When the wood is green, the shavings fly off in long ribbons. Turning green is quick and easy, and fun.

4 **Spoon shape.** Turn the spoon shape you want. The photo on page 31 shows some of the shapes I make. This blank had a bark inclusion, which I'll fill with epoxy as shown in Filling Defects.

5 **Jig.** A simple vee-block jig enables you to cut cylinders and spoons truly in half most of the time. Even with a jig, selecting where to cut the wood, to enhance the grain or to look after defects, remains a challenge.

Jig for Sawing Cylinders

To make this vee-block jig for the band saw, cut sheet material for a base platform about 30" (760mm) long and attach two 45-degree vee-blocks made by ripping a 2 x 4" (51mm x 102mm) in half. Saw into the jig and clamp it to the band-saw table.

If the turning is not a straight cylinder, mark it to establish its high point and as you cut through make sure that the turning does not rotate. A plywood square tacked to the end of the block will help keep things level and a V-block push stick will keep fingers clear. The only trouble left is a wandering saw blade and that means it needs to be changed for sharpening.

Safety. The push stick guides the blank along the jig and into the band-saw blade.

Carving

6 Draw a line. Draw a line where the bowl is to be carved. Even after many years of making the spoons I still draw the shape. To hold a spoon while carving, clamp it to a softwood vee-block but make sure the bowl is also supported on the bench.

7 Finish. Sand all the edges to increase the pleasure of handling and then apply a finish. I usually brush on mineral oil to saturate the wood. When making servers in larger numbers, I immerse them in a metal tub and prop them up on a drainage rack.

Finishing for Food

Mineral oil is safe for food. Avoid finishes like vegetable oil that eventually go rancid.

Mineral oil eventually evaporates or gets washed off and needs to be done again, though there is enough oil in the salad dressing we use to keep the spoons looking good and functioning well.

Mineral oil is prone to pick up dirt when handled from maker to shop to home, so the servers do need a good wash before use. When I started there were no satisfactory finishes for salad bowls or spoons, but now there are a number available. Read the labels carefully as some may be snake oil.

Mineral oil. Safe for food.

Filling Defects in the Wood

Sometimes there are flaws or bark inclusions in the wood, as shown in Step 4, so I clean them out and fill them with colored epoxy glue. It's a slow process, so the wood has to be very special visually or it has to have sentimental value for a client.

I usually use 5-minute epoxy colored with pigments I found at a marine supply store. These pigments are formulated for use with epoxy in fiberglass gel coats.

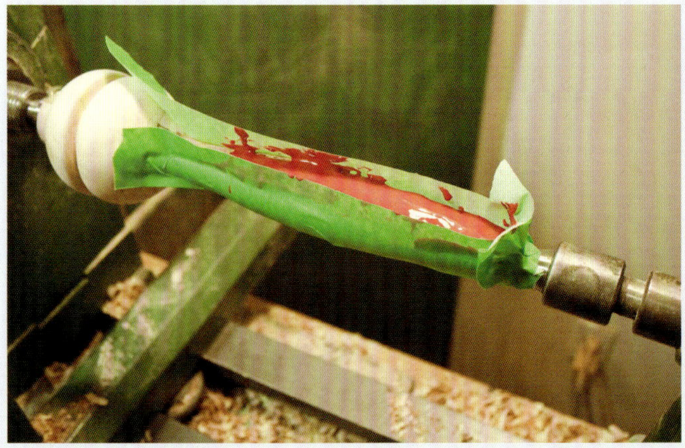

Filler. Green tape helps control the epoxy.

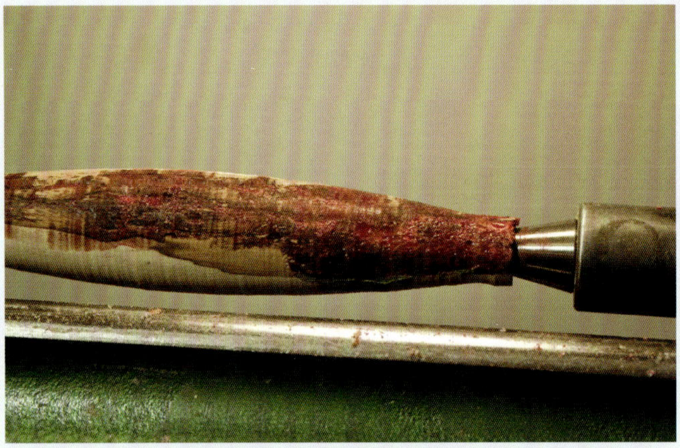

Turns clean. The wood and epoxy can be turned down with regular tools and sanded to a polish. Now all the bubbles and defects frustratingly show up.

Defects. The only thing you can do about bubbles and defects in the epoxy is to repeat the process.

More defects. Chances are when you cut the turning in half the flaws will show up again. Clean out the punky wood and apply more colored epoxy.

Avoid heat. I use files and also the belt sander for removing excess epoxy, though the machine is prone to heat the glue so it goes gummy and can pull out of the cavity. Go slowly to avoid heat build-up, and do not breath the epoxy dust.

Turnings for Sale

I usually set up to make ten pairs of servers at a time; it's efficient and the unit cost will go down. It's good to always sell what I make. The buyers for these have been easy to find, unlike some of my other designs. It has been helpful when work has been slow to have a production item to fall back on.

A word of caution if production is your direction. While shopping in the grocery store I stopped at a rather good $4 wood spoon for the kitchen. It was made from European beech, well finished with finely articulated edges, scoop, curves, and a comfortably long handle. The spoon was attached to a cardboard backing with printed information. I reflected on making one of these and then getting it into the store. First grow the tree, harvest the wood, and dry it. Shape and finish it and attach it to the card with a hole to hang it up. Then ship it across an ocean and truck it to a warehouse and on to the retailer. Someone must have gone broke.

The equipment needed to manufacture to this quality would be expensive, so thousands of spoons would have to be made to amortize the investment. Then you have to find the retailer. There were only four hanging on the rack at $4 each. Yikes, mine sell for close to $40! Different economics need different approaches, possibly a different look, even though the function may remain similar. The $4 spoon is anonymous whereas mine carry a richness in dimension with a hand carved element, and of course the important story about their source, whether it's from me or special wood from the client.

Three designs. I produce serving spoons in three designs: the classic shape that has a small cove for the elastic band that holds two spoons together; the designerly shape in the darker wood, and the blank cut into quarters to make slender spoons with a minimal bowl.

Limited Editions

These smaller form explorations from the 1970s were usually a turning cut in half or perhaps with an additional wedge removed. The wood forms were then taken to a foundry and cast in an alloy. They were sand-cast so the finish was basic and needed a lot of finishing, but the casting price was very good. I also poured clear and colored polyester resins into plaster molds made from the wood forms. The new flexible-rubber mold materials are very good and easy to work with. I made multiples of some; others remained sculptures. Round or sharp, designs like these have the potential for quite different configurations and uses. They may be hung on the wall, act as paperweights, bookends, or if you insist, door stops. The aluminum bowl with the painted black interior (bottom left) was manufactured in an unlimited edition in 1972.

Aluminum form.

Cast polyester resin.

Aluminum form.

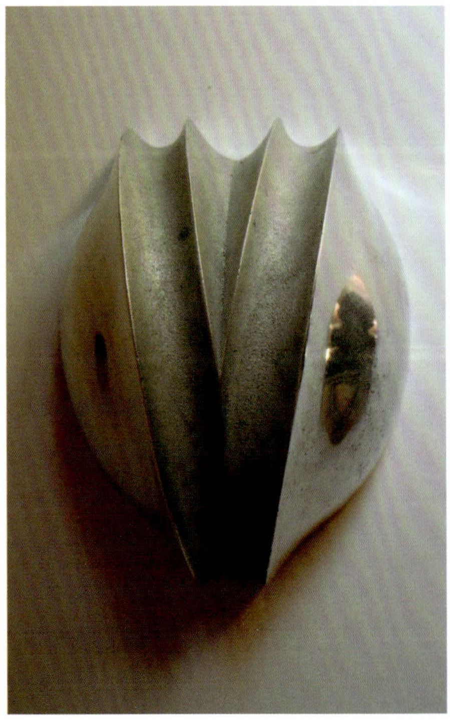

Aluminum form.

Table and Chairs

Split spindles

The chair and table are similar to the servers because the parts come from spindle turnings cut in half. The client was in England and after looking at crating and shipping I decided on a design I could carry over in my luggage. The six knock-down chairs were packed in two people's suitcases and assembled on site for the client. The economics worked better than crating and shipping and that was a huge reason for the construction and look of the furniture. The purpose was to sit at a table, but the shipping aspect gave me the aesthetic.

A year later I revisited the prototype chair and refined its arms (bottom photo); now it's with another collector. After hearing that it took seven years for an industrial designer to finalize an award-winning chair, I don't feel so bad about continuing to develop things in my sketchbook. More than one architect has said that it's more difficult to design a good chair than a good building. Doing it again will often yield refinements and improvements because it changes context. There are other ideas for this chair I would like to try, even though it was a great success for the original client.

COLLECTION: PRIVATE, LONDON, ENGLAND.

DAC Nomad Chair, 2006.
Ash, laminated wood, paint;
35" (890mm) x 23" (584mm)
x 22" (559mm).

COLLECTION: PRIVATE, OWEN SOUND, ONTARIO.

DAC prototype remodeled, 2007.
Ash, laminated wood, paint; 35" (890mm) x 23" (584mm) x 23" (584mm).

CHAPTER 3

Spindle turning, cut and rejoined

The Tree

Leaf motif evokes the green poplar

A neighbor cut down a poplar tree and thought I might like to turn a piece from it. Two billets arrived on my doorstep quite wet and fresh. They sat in my studio through most of the winter with my bonsai trees placed on top so the moisture came out slowly. Most poplar is not a great turning wood and ranges from Balm of Gilead, which is like turning cotton wool, to American poplar, which is quite a good-turning soft hardwood. This poplar was somewhere in the middle for density and I suspect it is balsam poplar. While I did not know the tree, I was very conscious of its treeness, partly because it was green wood and I had been thinking a lot about the importance of trees in my life.

I had started the Cornucopia chestnut piece (page 42), in which a vase or bowl shape is cut in half on its turning axis and reassembled rim-to-rim. I wanted to try green-turning something similar using the poplar. I am not really set up for deep bowl turning and should leave it to David Ellsworth. His technique is impeccable whereas mine will just see me through in a basic way.

Finishing the inside and outside took a while and other work distracted me. Returning weeks later, I wanted to find appropriate and meaningful colors and images for the bowl. I had begun with the idea of the Horn of Plenty, which brings images of desire, conjuring sensual pleasures with full, round and ripe fruit and delicate flowers freshly picked. But that put too many layers on this inquiry into the simple meaning of a piece of tree. I decided to paint the interior with the colors and forms of the poplar tree itself. Putting the tree back into the bowl expresses my desire and intention to plant some trees near my home this spring.

Rather than painting a realistic poplar, I was interested in an abstraction of trees. On reflection the piece may be seen as a bowl of seedlings to be planted. The necklace of the edge, painted red during the making but no longer red, still hangs about the trees as a symbol of life and renewal.

> "Making the joint work is critical to the re-joining of the fragments, so you need to think ahead to how the forms will fit, glue, and flow together."

PHOTO BY MICHAEL MCLUHAN

The Tree, 2011. Balsam poplar, 5" (127mm) x 29" (739mm) x 10" (457mm).

Turning The Tree

1 **Wood.** Mount the billet on the lathe with the centers exactly on the pith, which in this instance was close to the wood's center of mass so the billet was not too out of balance. Centering on the pith reduces checking by removing the unstable juvenile wood.

2 **Rough turn.** Turn the bark off with a large gouge. There were spalting lines and stains in the wood, probably because it sat around for a long time. No problem—I like the marks found in wood.

3 **The blank.** The piece has been turned down to make the blank, which is the canvas on which the design will develop. The billet is now as balanced as it will get, so the lathe speed can be higher for the finer cuts.

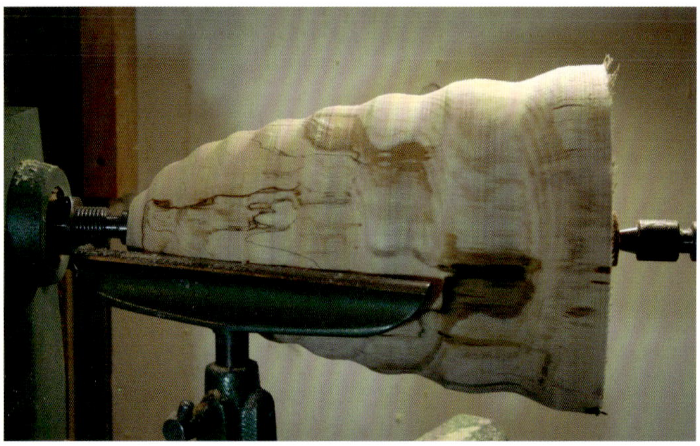

4 **Develop ribs.** Use a spindle gouge or a round-end scraper to develop the ribs of the Horn of Plenty. With green wood, let the turned blank sit overnight before sanding so surface moisture can evaporate.

5 **Scrape inside.** Turn out the inside using a scraper. I try not to sand inside because the sanding would distort the roundness and make the halves not fit together so well. Making the joint work is critical to the re-joining of the fragments, so think ahead to how the forms will fit, glue, and flow together.

Sawing the turning apart

6 **Safety.** Sawing into something round can be difficult and dangerous because the saw is liable to grab the wood and maybe break the blade. Make a carriage to hold and control the workpiece. Here I am nailing a piece of plywood onto one end.

7 **Support.** At the other end I've attached another piece of plywood using a screw. It's important to remember, when cutting it in half, to stop before hitting the screw.

8 **Saw through.** The big band saw slices through the plywood supports and on down to within an inch of the screw. On a smaller saw table, you would fasten the plywood supports to a sacrificial base of plywood or MDF.

9 **Last cut.** Remove the plywood supports and all metal, and use a hand saw to cut the last two inches. Turnings can be cut apart with nothing but a hand saw and that's how I started, but a band saw is just incredibly useful for this operation.

10 **End angle.** The two halves laid end to end reveal my poor turning technique. This also shows the angle at which the ends need to be sawn so the halves can fit together (Step 11).

The Mystique of the Wood Bowl

Cleaning up the inside of the bowl forces consideration of the edge shape. As I carved, the edge reminded me of a necklace so I painted the edge bright red to help me see and develop this idea (later I planed the red paint off). The Brisingamen necklace is an evocative image in the Nordic tradition and in Egyptian mythology where the Menet Necklace, associated with the god Halthor, represents life, potency, fertility, birth, and renewal. Rather a lot for a simple wood bowl to carry, but the container has always had the mystique of high potential. After all, the cornucopia and Horn of Plenty also promise a great deal.

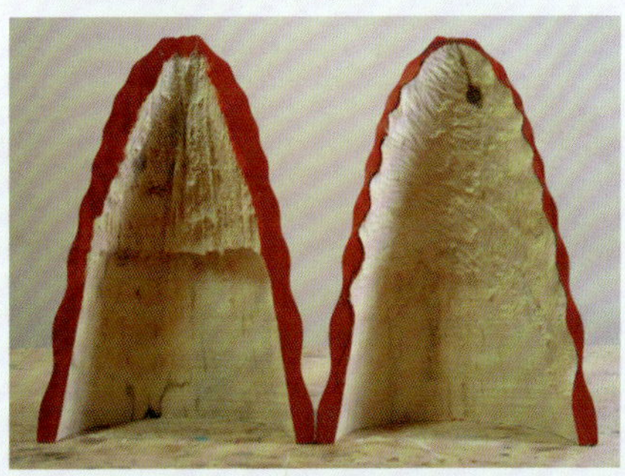

Red necklace.

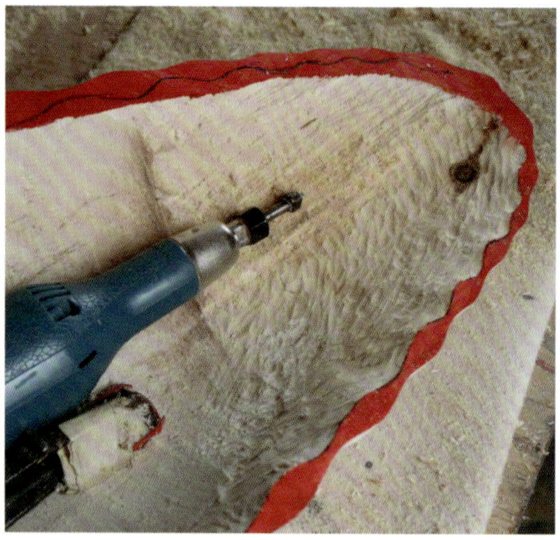

11 **Saw angle.** With the bulk of the waste material removed, the end of the bowl can be sawn on an angle. Set the band-saw table at the angle and clamp a guide close to the blade. Push the wood along the edge of the guide.

12 **Carve.** Use a die grinder or carving gouges to clean up the inside of the bowl while you develop the interior shape and the edge. Painting the edge helps you see the shape as you carve.

13 **Explore.** It's always fun and interesting to explore the possible arrangements of the two halves. This will help generate ideas for using similar forms in other projects. Along with the sketchbook (page 50), the camera is a terrific tool for recording ideas.

Joining End-Grain

Joining end-grain to end-grain is always a challenge. Glue alone will join side-grain to side-grain, but end-grain needs reinforcement.

This bowl has three wood pins and good-quality water-resistant PVA glue. I use small nails to align the holes. With three nails in one half, you can slide the two halves together (step 15) to leave matching marks in both. Take care to set up the drill press for accurate holes where the nails left dimples (below left). It's possible to do it by eye but really difficult to get perfect alignment (center).

Clamp the two halves together if possible. The turned form is invariably tricky to clamp but occasionally, as with this piece, the pressure is in exactly in the right place (below right). Glue it together as soon as possible after turning and let the glue set at least overnight.

Drill for the dowels.

Take care with alignment.

Glue and clamp.

Putting it together

14 **The bowl.** Here's the two bowl halves put together as I intended. As I took this photograph the edge appeared as a necklace, which I liked (see page 37, The Mystique of the Wood Bowl).

15 **Join.** Getting alignment and a good glue joint on end-grain is tricky, but essential. The length of this bowl increases the potential stress on the joint, so I inserted three wood dowels as reinforcement (see Joining End-Grain). Another strategy would be to emphasize the joint and make its reinforcement a feature.

16 **Surface.** Clean out the interior using every tool in the workshop. Turning an accurate form up front is better than grinding the shape and your teeth to reach perfection. However you do it, you have to get to a surface and finish appropriate for the concept and form.

17 **Sand.** The sanding was endless so I gave up my plan for a painted edge with clear wood interior, and decided to paint the whole inside. To make an abstraction of trees, I changed the scale of trunk to leaf and used paint to fill the bowl with the green wonder of the woods.

Paint and Color

I paint the interiors of bowls to resolve the finishing problems, plus I really like the color contrast with wood and I enjoy the painting itself. I don't want an industrial-looking surface; I prefer the look of the hand at work.

When I began to paint I decided to work with water-based acrylic house paints. I had a bunch of half filled cans of various colors. Both on grounds of economy and of concern for the environment, I diluted the paints and applied them sparingly, brushing them on thinly to go further. The previously applied color showed through, so the colors interacted. I found it was possible to achieve great depth in the finish in this way and it helped me to leave further behind the cold, flat finishes and "perfection" of factory production.

With many of the cans empty, skinned over, or caked up, I think I was kidding myself about using small amounts of paint. I decided to adopt artists' acrylics. They have finely ground pigments and many colors, are easy to mix, and are readily available in small quantities. When looked after, the jars of paint last a long time; some of my colors not used often are now decades old and still in good condition. I have looked at other makers' results with milk paint, sometimes feeling a bit envious, but have stuck with this developed system. When durability in service is a requirement, I varnish over the acrylic with clear semigloss or satin polyurethane varnish, using a brush on larger objects and a spray can on smaller ones. It brings up the color without changing it. The oil-based urethane is easier to sand between coats but it's possible to get a good finish with water-based as well.

Start with the three primary colors of red, yellow and blue. Experiment with mixing the colors together. Add some black to shade or darken and white to tint or lighten. Then get the secondary colors as you can afford them. If you like pure color, the manufacturers can make it better than you can mix it. As you build your palette there are gold and silver iridescent glazes that will add some sparkle. There are huge variations possible and that can become a problem. When starting out with color, work with adjacent colors so if the main color is red mix a little yellow in to get a red/yellow (orange) on one side and a little blue to make a red/blue (violet) on the other side. They become the same or analogous, while still having their own similar characteristics. Always keep a color chart handy to help you think what the relationships are about.

Paint resolves finishing problems.

The color chart helps you find analogous colors (adjacent to one another) and complementary colors (across from one another).

CHAPTER 4

Faceplate turning, cut and rejoined

Chestnut Cornucopia

Turned shapes work with wood layers

It was a sad day when the horse chestnut tree had to come down to make way for the extension of my studio workshop. In the spring the flowers were magnificent and the sound of bees more than once left me wondering what machine was running in the distance. But the tree was diseased from a blight of the leaves, which turned brown and fell as the summer progressed. The chestnuts were prolific in the fall, attracting chipmunks, squirrels and me collecting seeds to grow more trees for other parts of the property.

The tree was cut into one-inch and two-inch thick boards about nine feet long, and stacked to air-dry for three years. I planned to build up the blank for the bowl by gluing layers of chestnut together. I would turn a bowl, them saw it in half and glue the two pieces together rim to rim. I wanted the shape to work with the glue lines so the structure and the finished look would work together. The wood for the bowl was to come from a 9′ (2743mm) x 14" (356mm) x 2" (51mm) board, not fully wide enough for the large piece I had in mind, but more than wide enough for semicircles. The board tapered, which became a feature of the finished bowl—the Horn of Plenty does of course taper. The tapering also suggested a change of thickness for each layer, easy enough with the thickness planer.

I first made bowls like this in 1975, when I spent a year in Australia. I remember making it from King Billy pine (shown below) and at that time mulling over the idea of cornucopia and the Horn of Plenty. *Copia* is the Latin word for abundance, plenty, and multitude. Copia was a Roman goddess probably associated with the harvest and copied from the nature harvest goddess Ops. The image for the Horn of Plenty derives from a fight between Hercules and Amalthea, who had turned himself into a bull. Hercules breaks the horn from the bull and it is later filled with fruit and flowers, and sanctified.

The finished piece sits tall, rippling with energy, not exactly a horn because the original board was only nine feet long. It is shocking that so much material reduces to such a small form. The original form of the Horn of Plenty was the inspiration, but the actual plank of wood and the work led the way to something new. The material from the horse chestnut tree talked back, and yet when filled with fruit and flowers it is just as desirable. This piece was shipped out to the 2011 SOFA exhibition in Chicago and then went on to be shown at the American Association of Woodturners Gallery of Wood Art in St. Paul.

PHOTO BY TONY BOYD

Bowl, 1975. King Billy pine, 16" (39cm) long.

PHOTO BY MICHAEL MCLUHAN

Cornucopia, 2011.
Horse chestnut,
8" (203mm) x
18" (457mm) x
17" (432mm).

"It is shocking that so much material reduces to such a small form."

Preparing the material

1 **Wood.** The pieces of wood vary in width and thickness, making the most of the tapering plank from the chestnut tree. The thickness planer skimmed the surface and the semicircles I had drawn on the wood. Cut off the first length, plane again, cut again.

2 **Semicircles.** Cut out the semicircles using the band saw. Here's how the stack will go together for turning. The last pieces came from a thinner plank.

3 **Glue.** A very wise woodworker named Bruno Armelin once told me to glue only two boards at a time. If there are connecting pins to stop the boards from sliding around then you might do more layers at one time. But the advice to go slow has always kept me out of glue-up trouble.

4 **Clamp.** Glue the boards together using a waterproof PVA glue. Clamp the stacks to the work table while the glue sets.

5 **Join.** Clean the glue off and flatten the two halves to glue them together for turning. Glue paper into the joint if you don't have a big band saw to cut the block apart later. Glue a small plywood disk on top and bottom, for the lathe centers.

Turning the form

6 **Safety.** Glue a wooden tab across the joint on both sides of the form to help keep it together. Bad things do happen: the dent in the wall just above the tailstock lever was made by a solid-wood turning that flew apart. and ran up the wall into the ceiling.

7 **Turn the outside.** Turn down the outside, responding to the glue lines, to make the form. Sand for the final finish.

8 **Turn the inside.** I use heavy scraping tools to turn out the interior; a bowl gouge would work as well if you have skill with that.

9 **Support.** Leave the central stem for tailstock support. Make the stem thinnest at the bottom of the form, so it's easy to break away later.

10 **Finish end.** Refine the end of the turning on the outside, to minimize the amount of handwork later. Remove the bowl from the lathe.

11 **Break stem.** Whack the stem inside the bowl to break it off. With some luck the wood will break in just the right place. Here the break went deeper than I wanted, but it was not an issue because I planned to cut the form and hand-shape it.

Splitting the turning

12 **Cut apart.** If you used a paper joint you can split it apart, though the glue will have to be removed and that may be an ugly job. Even with a paper joint, I prefer to band saw the piece because the cut removes the glue and leaves a clean wood surface.

13 **What angle?** Look at the two halves and see how they may go together. At what angle should the form rest? Use small blocks to prop it up to different angles. Keeping the two halves separate for now makes it easier to clamp them to the bench while you work on the details.

14 **Shape.** Cut the shape out with a coping saw, then use a sanding drum, a Surform, and rasps to shape the wood. While working I am thinking about the best shape to articulate the action of pouring.

15 **Saw end.** Propping up the pieces as in Step 13 shows that a wedge needs to be removed from what was the rim of the turned bowl. If it's a large cut, use the band saw; a small wedge could be sanded off on the disk sander.

Joining the fragments

16 **Look.** Having removed the wedge, pause to study the parts. Invariably some surprises happen. The wedge looks like it could be a horn. The bowl is giving back the Horn of Plenty in a different form. Perhaps these fragments will become another piece.

17 **Flatten.** To flatten the mating surfaces, I use a large shop-made sanding disk running slowly on the lathe. The slow speed is incredibly helpful: the piece is not ripped out of your hands and your fingertips are spared the risk of being sanded down to the bone. The disk will get close to a finished flat plane.

18 **Smooth.** Do the final sanding on a flat board with glued-down 100-grit paper. Hold the piece firmly and be careful to not rock it. Sand both halves, place them together, and look for light coming through the joint. It's tricky to get it perfect but it is possible.

19 **Join.** Glue and clamp the piece together. Be careful—too much pressure can distort the wood and wreck the carefully prepared gluing surfaces. Always align the inside rather than the outside, because the inside is much more difficult to clean up.

20 **Sand.** Leave the piece for 24 hours for the glue to completely set, then sand the joint to clean it up and make a fair surface. The small disk sander is a big help, though hand-sanding is usually needed to get the final finish.

21 **Color.** Painting the interior is about applying layer upon layer. The texture from the brush gives it a loose and warm look. Finishing with a good quality semi-gloss polyurethane varnish seals the surface, making it water-resistant and possible to wipe clean.

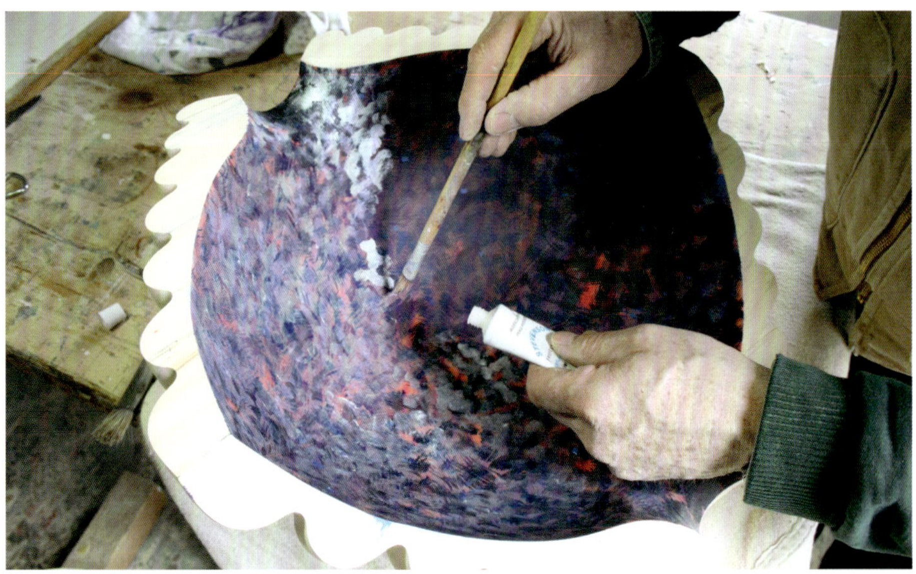

Daydreaming Generates New Ideas

The pattern of the stacked boards resembles a spiral staircase. As I become immersed in my work a dream-like state may take hold. It is like daydreaming, and while the purpose of the object is not lost, the mind makes random associations. What else might this shape, this stack of boards, become?

It's useful to pause to make sketches and take photographs to record ideas.

Further investigation may be fruitful, or not. I'm intrigued by these spiral patterns, and I made a number of pieces using them. But after making the red cedar bowl in the photo below, I had to conclude that it was too time-consuming. I've since seen others make good use of forms like these, so it's often about roads not taken.

COLLECTION: PRIVATE, CHEARSLEY, UK.

Playing with blocks. The stack resembles a staircase.

COLLECTION: PRIVATE, TORONTO.

Spiral Bowl, 1973. Western red cedar; 15" (381mm) dia.

COLLECTION: PRIVATE, CHEARSLEY, UK.

Spiral Form, 1972. Pine; 15" (381mm) dia.

COLLECTION: PRIVATE, CHEARSLEY, UK.

Spiral Form, 1972. Pine; 15" (381mm) dia.

Opening the Bowl

1970s

I was trained as an industrial designer but I have avoided industry and instead make my living as a designer-maker. The sequence of cut forms happened over decades, one step at a time. I enjoyed a rush of creative exploration in the first five years, and the sketchbooks show many drawings of alternative designs. Many of these early designs were looking at nature not for decorative ideas like Art Nouveau, but for structural ideas about the way things work.

The early plates and bowls were made on a faceplate and then cut up. I was fascinated by the fluid cross-sections and soon discovered asymmetries within the symmetry of the lathe. The relationship between the inside and outside of the form, revealed by the flowing edge, was absorbing. Forms like these are easily achieved in turned wood, unlike in ceramics or cast metal. These forms seem unique to wood.

I often wondered about making bowls out of spindle turnings and the Ceremonial Bowl (photo at bottom right on page 51) was the first in 1976. But it wasn't until 2000 that I started making the dancing bowls (page 52) from spindle turnings.

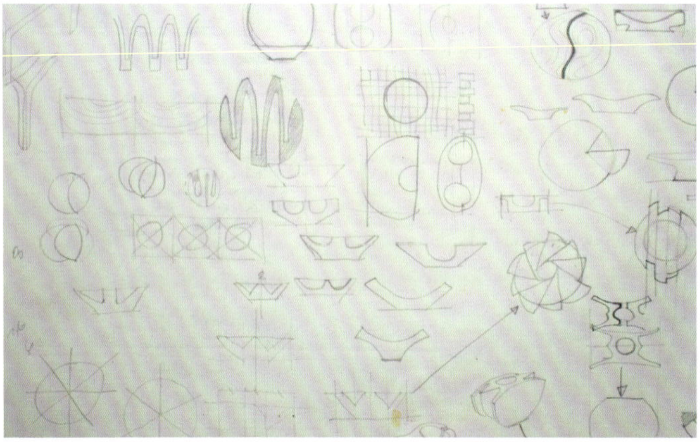

Sketchbooks from the 1970s show a rush of exploration in the universe of bowl forms.

Fluid Clam, 1972. American walnut, 11" (279mm) x 5½" (140mm).

COLLECTION: PRIVATE, OAKVILLE, ONTARIO.

Early sale

My colleague at Sheridan College, the late Don McKinley, saw Fluid Clam and was perplexed by its fluid form because it was unable to contain anything except its own space. I explained my interest in the natural forms of fluids floating together, like oil on water or air trapped in ice. The curving lines, while not exactly structural, do show the interaction of one substance to another. Apart from those interests, it was at the time a difficult form to create and it shows off the new techniques I was developing. It is, as David Pye would say, "the difference between useless and ineffectual." The form may be useless like laughter or flowers, but it's not ineffectual to woodworkers. McKinley purchased the piece, which was high praise in the early years when I wondered where these strange new forms would take me.

COLLECTION: PRIVATE, TORONTO, ONTARIO.

Asymetrical Turned Bowl, 1972. Mahogany, 13" (330mm) dia.

Asymmetrical bowl

Two plates are turned with the same diameter but different cross sections. They are joined at the rim to make a hollow and enclosed form. Next the piece is cut in half through the center. One half was left as the exact half, and the other half was cut back to give the top a sympathetic curve (shown). This piece has a poetic flow throughout the form, whereas the exact half retained the hard geometry of the process.

Another look

The piece at right is from a series of bowls that stood on end. There were some practical reasons, like storage of the piece in a cupboard, but really it was the chance to see the form in another way. The work takes on a very different character when it's presented away from its function. It's the oldest trick for artists to stand things on their metaphoric head to get a fresh view of what's going on. The other part of this piece that interested me was the possibility of including handles by which to carry the bowl. The idea of carrying the bowl to the table or presenting it to another so they may serve themselves is the precursor to the Ceremonial Bowl I made in Australia (bottom right). The purpose of the object often contains multiple ideas. A piece will change quite dramatically according to the context in which it's placed or how it's presented.

COLLECTION: PRIVATE, TORONTO, ONTARIO.

Untitled, 1974. Red oak, 19.75" (483mm) x 11" (279mm) dia.

Spindle bowl

The Australian turner and educator Vic Wood delivered a very special piece of wood to the studio workshop at Melbourne State College when I was craftsman in residence there. He explained it was grass tree from a road widening project and very difficult wood to get because it was now a protected species. It was with great care that I made a ceremonial bowl (right) that could be used. There are many small objects that have a big function in the drama of living, and while wood is the humblest material used for these occasions it may well become more significant as the environment gets spoiled. Cultures that have less of any single resource will invariably give the material a special place in the ritual of life. This piece also has technical significance in that it was the first bowl I had made from a spindle turning instead of off the faceplate.

COLLECTION: PRIVATE, MELBOURNE, AUSTRALIA.

Ceremonial Bowl, 1976. Grass tree, 19" (483mm) x 10" (254mm) dia.

Bowls from Spindles

2000s

Finally, a satisfactory series started to develop using spindle turning to make a new fragmented bowl. Cutting them into four or laminating four blanks together is easier than three pieces. Three legs do stand square on the floor. The four-piece configuration does leave a hole in the center as the parts are adjusted or realigned; it may be filled with an additional block or left open. Easy to turn, these forms are difficult to glue together. Two of the forms shown are sedate, with one standing, the other walking, and the third quite actively dancing.

Look at the foot

There were a number of designs that investigated the foot of the bowl. Some of the bowls were long-legged with the proportions of a spider, while Tulip Bowl had the character of the opening tulip.

Floral forms

During my 2002 residency at the Australian National University there was a wonderful photographic exhibition of flower images. One of them was a close up that gave the view a bee would see. I was enchanted with the pattern and idea of that proximity, and there was a piece of rose alder under the bench just waiting to be turned. It all fell into place and this piece became one of my favorites from the series.

Run for your life

How fast will the bowl appear to move? (right). Sculpture was initially quite static, but through the centuries movement became more apparent. How to free the stasis of material and animate the form was most sought after by the Futurists. Speed was ever-present in their work and these days many try to reverse that trend into the slow movement, while looking for the limits of growth. Running from the future is futile, but speed and growth are probably the major issues for Western culture. Our success, perhaps our survival, will depend on how we run with the environment.

COLLECTION: THE ARTIST.

What the Bees Saw, 2002. Rose alder, paint, 13" (330mm) x 8" (203mm).

COLLECTION: THE ARTIST.

Running Bowl, 2001. Walnut, paint; 9" (229mm) high x 10" (254mm).

Tulip Bowl, 2001. Red elm, paint, 12" (305mm) x 7" (178mm) dia.

CHAPTER 5

Faceplate turning, cut and rejoined

Platter

Managing wood with wild grain

The cherry log arrived at my studio workshop carefully chained down on the back of a trailer. Quietly I thought, "Oh my god it grew in a spiral." The nuclear engineer and his partner had driven many miles with the log from their front lawn and I felt that I could not just say, "No thanks."

Wood with wild grain and figure is often referred to as "character" wood. It's full of swirls, knots, and perhaps bark inclusions. Some people find such wood just ugly; they may prefer plain, straight, subtle, understated, or refined grain. In this plate project, the cherry's wild grain takes over the form and becomes the predominant idea behind the piece. At the start, I intended to make an eye shape of the two halves, to present a contrast between hard and soft, but on this occasion the wild grain eclipsed that idea and the flow of the wood figure became the dominant idea. The grain eddies around the knots and through the form. Perhaps now that I am older, ideas of flow have become more important when looking at relationships, whether human or otherwise.

One of my early turnings from 1971 was a plate that had a honeycomb check from poor kiln drying, which became a hairline crack at its center. I decided to cut out the crack and glue the pieces together to make an eye shape (page 57). With the form cut apart, the cross-section suggested other ways of putting it back together. I saw the two fragments as full of potential where two halves may make a whole. At the time I was recently married with a child on the way and I saw in the plate the coming together of many possibilities. How much do the relationships we have influence our perception and then our creative work?

Some of the best ideas come at times when emotions are high, which is another way of being fully alert and focused. For the maker, the struggle is with framing the problem or articulating the desire, having more than one idea, selecting the right design, and finding appropriate materials. The cut-apart plate from 1971 could have been thrown away but early on I learned to turn problems into an advantage. The material may just demand to be made a certain way, especially if it's wood. Who is in control? Well, it's a symbiotic push and pull between the concept for the piece and what the materials suggest or even demand.

"How do you know what's going on inside a piece of wood?"

PHOTO BY MICHAEL MCLUHAN

Plate, 2011. Cherry, 16" dia.

"The wood may just demand to be made a certain way."

Preparing the material

1 **Twisty wood.** Trees that grow in a spiral tend to create boards that want to go into a spiral, certainly boards that look like a propeller.

2 **Losing the wane.** Here I'm looking for the relationship among the knots. Because I planned to remove the center from the turning, I could keep the wane edge and the bark to the inside. What will happen after the piece is turned is unknown; however, I do know the wood is unpredictable and will do what it wants.

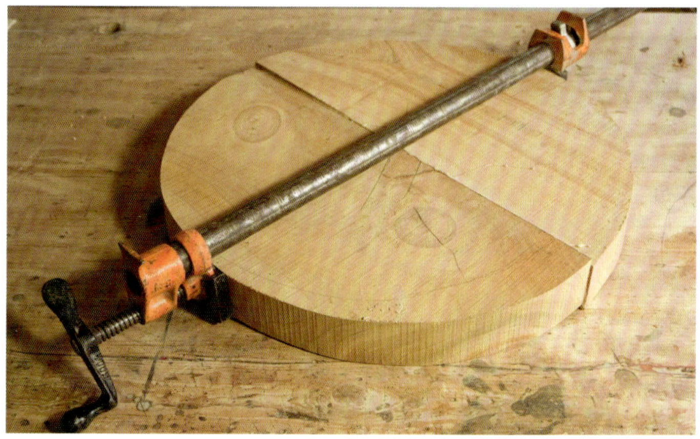

3 **Saw semicircles.** The boards were so warped they had to be cut into a semicircle before gluing together with regular PVA glue. I stepped the two semicircles to help manage the twist.

4 **Plywood disk.** Plane the center flat so you can center and glue a plywood disk onto it. The stair-steps at the edge will be turned down.

5 **Faceplate.** Screw a metal faceplate onto the plywood disk. Later on the plywood will be easy to split off the workpiece.

Turning the plate

6 **Front side.** True the front and turn the front of the plate. I prefer scraping tools, but the bowl gouge will also do this job.

7 **Foot side.** True up the back, and think about the size of the foot. Too small and the plate will not balance well in use. Too large and it will look clumsy.

Cut and glue

8 **Eye shape.** Now off the lathe, the center of the plate will be removed to get rid of the wane edge and develop the eye shape. It is a simple cut on the band saw, making sure the wood is properly supported, which might mean flipping the workpiece upside-down.

9 **Square edges.** I experimented with the fragments (see Magic of the Cross Section, page 59), but then, wanting to keep it simple, I planed the edges square to the face.

10 **Listen.** With the cut-outs sketched on the wood, I decided to leave the sawing until later, to have more time to think it through. The animated wood figure is calling for some specific shapes. It's talking back and when this happens it is essential to hear what the piece has to say.

11 **Glue.** A good joint needs only light pressure with a fine bead of glue squeeze-out running its full length. This plate clamped perfectly, but sometimes it's difficult to apply pressure without having the pieces flip open. Extended open-time glue is a godsend.

12 **Saw shape.** Cut out the shape on the band saw, scroll saw, or with a coping saw. Clean up the edge with rasps and the drum sander on the drill. For an almost sanded surface, finish up with a mill file.

Epoxy fills voids

13 **Color.** The cherry had a bark inclusion and minor checks from drying, which I filled with colored epoxy. I use regular 5-minute epoxy colored with gel-coat pigments that I got from a marine supplier.

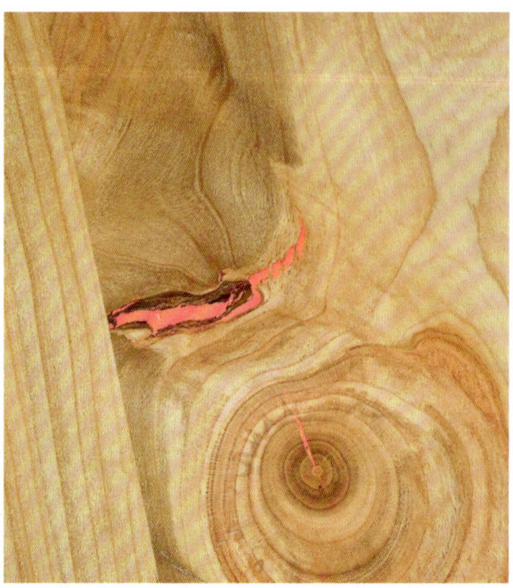

14 **Contrasts.** The epoxy makes a strong contrast with the figure in the wood. There is no way to conceal a check this big—better to emphasize it, make a feature of it.

Fit the Inside

Always get the joint fitting best on the inside of the plate or bowl because the inside can be very difficult to clean up. The back or bottom is easy to work over with files and abrasives.

The better it fits on the inside, the less sanding.

Magic of the Cross Section

Whenever I cut into a woodturning I like to try the pieces in different orientations and look at the magic of the cross-section. It is like cutting an apple in half or opening a geode to reveal the inner structure. The myriad ways the fragments could go back together never fail to surprise and delight me. This cutting up perhaps goes back as far as art school: I recall cutting up a cabbage while looking for design ideas. There was no particular goal in mind, it was just looking at nature with curiosity and marveling at the patterns of growth. I remember the cabbage and my attempt to draw its cross section, but I have no recollection of what I did with the revelation. Just experiencing life will spill into whatever you are working on.

I've also learned that transforming what is experienced into a project that works takes endless practice, one step at a time. The mind has to be trained to make connections. As children we do it naturally and then probably have to relearn how to do it as adults.

The cross section reveals the profile of a piece and lets me know what's going on inside. The weight of the object is often determined by its cross section. When thin it seems to float and is feather-light, while a heavy cross section will give the piece heft and help it remain grounded. The words describe a physical presence that also translates to a visual character. Revealing the cross section also opens up two interacting lines or edges, one on the inside and the other on the outside. The cross section looks at inside - outside relationships and how they flow together. The relationship between our interior experience and the exterior world is a metaphor for life and what we all do all the time to survive. Ceramic objects need parallel lines and a uniform thickness of clay for the firing process, but woodturnings may move from thick to thin, with swelling and pulsating profiles. The cross section is more like a crossroads where a junction, an intersection, and cross-referencing may occur. It is incredibly rich physical and visual territory. The cross section inevitably opens up an idea. Opening the physical form to what end? It always has the potential to be revelatory.

The cross section is further explored in the trivet project, page 62.

Try it this way...

...try it that way...

...and try it some other way.

Following the Grain

The plate with the human figure shows one of my earliest faceplate turnings from 1971. The circle was interrupted by cutting in alignment with the grain. The two bites were part of a circle so it's a play between three circles. The piece was made from elm and is quite small. The photo is an illusion created by the figure cut from a magazine picture, which changes the scale of the plate. Early on in my explorations, scale became an issue. How big is a turning?

The second photo shows the first plate that I cut in half to remove a honeycomb check, also from 1971. It had a fine check that only showed as I started the turning. With the plate finished, the check was removed and then came the revelation that the plate could be put back together in a variety of ways. More on that in Magic of the Cross Section, page 59.

Grain lines. Cutting along the wood figure interrupts the turned circle in this early turning from 1971.

Remove defect. Cutting the honeycomb check out of this plate opens a world of new possibilities.

Regional Woods, Forest Renewal

I prefer to work with regional woods such as maple, ash, oak, beech, and others that grow near the Great Lakes. Using regional woods is better for the environment and the price is about value within my community rather than the cost of shipping. The arguments for sustainability are well understood and, fortunately, more people are moving toward doing the right thing. The forests from my region have supported a furniture industry for more than a century. In the 1950s the government realized just how valuable the resource was and over the subsequent decades has been supporting the renewal of forests. It's not been without controversy, but the environment has become a vital part of the public discourse. The small operator caring for all aspects of harvesting and manufacturing locally has to be the way forward.

It took many years before I had a wood lot on my own property that might deliver lumber of significant dimensions. It's not really practical to grow the tree, harvest it and convert it to lumber, air dry the boards, and then make something for a client. A commission usually has to happen quickly, so I go to a supplier such as A&M Wood Specialty to source the materials I need and the project moves ahead. The wood lot, on the other hand, has trees felled at a particular time of year and the wood must be put up to dry for one to three years. I have also worked with lumber from a farmer across the lake who has a magnificent wood lot. Speculative work I make for exhibition often features the wood from Lake Charles, Ontario, where I live.

COLLECTION: THE ARTIST.

Untitled, 1974. Elm, 13" (330mm) dia. x 25" (635mm) x 3" (76mm).

COLLECTION: PRIVATE, TORONTO.

Plate, 1971. Elm, 9" (229mm) dia.

COLLECTION: PRIVATE, OAKVILLE, ONTARIO.

Plate, 1971. Maple, 11" (279mm) dia.

Plate, 1971. Elm, 7" (178mm) dia.

COLLECTION: PRIVATE, VANCOUVER.

Plate, 1971. Maple, 11" (279mm) dia.

COLLECTION: MELBOURNE UNIVERSITY, AUSTRALIA.

Table, 1976. Mountain grey gum. 27" (685mm) dia. x 27" (685mm).

CHAPTER 6

Faceplate turning, many cuts

Trivet or Sculpture

Cross section reveals flowing curves

Instead of a single cut, the turning for this trivet is cut multiple times into strips, which are then rearranged. The number of potential arrangements is considerable. Before starting the cross section needs to be determined, and turned wood is unique among craft processes in being able to display, in the cross section, an enticingly curvaceous line (see Magic of the Cross Section, page 59).

"Trivet" is related to "trivial" and is often associated with the meeting of three roads or three ways. Trivets are for hot plates, bowls, and other utensils. The association of coming together and a hot connection is satisfying. The meeting of three increases complexity over a meeting of two. So the trivet has a noble past from the meeting of the ways, and the trivial or mundane is always hot at the center of the table.

I am interested in ideas of flow. Water is the best analogy but air would come into the idea as well. In my early designs the ideas of oil on water or air being trapped in ice have quite specific fluid curves that I found particularly attractive. The meeting of two rivers and how they would flow together also has a rich meaning: the meeting of different elements, how they interact and the patterns they make in two and three dimensions. In this design the curves are generated from the turned circle by cutting it into strips. The overall pattern becomes like the ripples on water and cloud formations. The patterning is satisfyingly attached to chaos theory. Out of this simple object many ideas flow, and it's a useful metaphor for designing. The designer can have self, subject, object, and context flow together in the process of making this trivet.

And, in fact, in the process of developing this project, I did get to the trivet I had intended to make, Step 7. But as I reviewed the work I realized that although attractive, this is an impractical trivet. Made of wood, a hot pan may well burn it. When food is spilled on it, how can it be cleaned? It would need to be cast in plastic or aluminum so it could take the heat and be hosed down. At the meeting of the ways through material, form, and function, the piece fails. But it is not a total disaster; finding its value and turning a failure to our advantage is equally important. I followed the path onward to make a wall piece using the fragments of the turning.

Technically, it would be possible to make this design from two solid blocks glued together. The block once turned would then be cut up on the table saw, but there is a loss of material and it's more difficult to clean up. I preferred to prepare the material in the form of square sticks that could be clamped together on the lathe in a work-holding fixture—and even so, by the end of this project I had sawn each prepared strip into two. Usually I can use off-cuts from other projects, in this instance from staircase treads which, when finished on all faces, measured out to 1¼" (32mm) square by 16" (406mm) long. I prefer a tight-grained hardwood like maple, birch, or cherry. This time I used ash, knowing some parts would be painted. This is a large project requiring a large lathe or the ability to turn outboard, but you can scale it to the equipment, and scrap wood, that you have.

> "The trivial or mundane is always hot at the center of the table."

PHOTO BY MICHAEL MCLUHAN

Bluewater Trivet, 2012.
Ash, acrylic paint,
16" x 32"

Turning the disk

1 **Template.** The cross section has been designed and drawn on thick cardboard. Cut out the card using a knife or jig saw, and keep the scrap pieces. Glue the cardboard template in between the center strips of wood. When the assembly is on the lathe, turn it down to the shaped cardboard.

2 **Fixture.** Mount the fixture on the lathe. Number the work-holding parts so if the piece has to be made again it's possible to reassemble the fixture.

3 **Mark.** Mark out the high points by observing the cardboard template buried between the strips. You can't see the template when turning, so the lathe will be switched on and off many times in the process.

4 **External template.** An external template, using the scrap from making the internal one, also may be offered up to the workpiece. Keeping all parts of the template does enable you to go both ways as you turn both sides of the square.

First trivet

5 Paint. After turning, the surface could be painted with a color, but I prefer to disassemble the pieces and look at the pattern first. These surfaces are painted with an undercoat as it helps to see the pattern more clearly. The difference between natural wood and painted surface enhances the flickering and rippling effect.

6 Assemble. Here's one way of putting it back together, but there are many more (see On Fragmented Turnings, page 68).

7 Glue. I liked this arrangement and decided to use blue color to enhance the association with water. We could quit at this point, clean up the strips, and glue it together, and it would make a trivet for the center of a table.

Pushing further

8 More strips. I wanted more pieces to work with so I cut each strip in half down its length. This doubles the length of the piece from 16" (406mm) square to 16" x 32" (406mm x 812mm)—a large trivet, perhaps for a large table.

9 Another pattern. As the sticks are cut and stacked off to the side, the stack falls over and another pattern presents itself. The ripples push closer again to water.

Making it glow

10 **Wet look.** The surface of the blue is a matte acrylic and it needs a wet look. In the past I have used iridescent paint and this time I am trying a "spectral color, rainbow" which contains many colored reflective particles.

11 **Movement.** Up close it looks a bit raw but standing back it glows with wetness. The smallest shift activates the movement and feeling of waves. Wait and see just how all the finished pieces will look.

12 **Another pattern.** The strips were in pairs when cleaned off with abrasives. This is the pattern of sanding dust left behind, suggesting other possible ideas for generating new forms.

Trivet or wall sculpture?

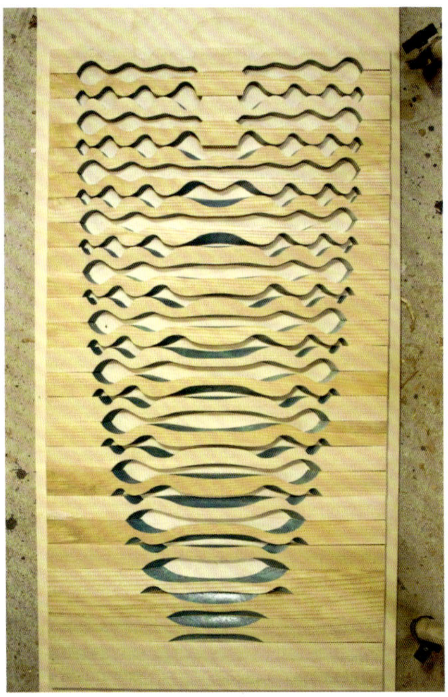

13 **Decisions.** Here are the sticks in three different arrangements. Should it become a wall hanging, a table centerpiece, remain a trivet, or perhaps become both? What makes a great trivet? Discovering the piece could be laid on the table or hung on the wall added onto the original intention.

14 More color. The piece was looking wooden so I decided to add a colored backing. In mosaics the colored grout brings harmony and unity to object and background.

15 Light glows. Where I live, the lakes are crystal clear and the colors in the water are truly fabulous. I started with bottle green, then a black wash for the depths of water. Start with thin coats of the lightest and brightest colors and then knock them back with successive layers. The light seems to glow from the surface.

Jig for Holding Strips

A false faceplate is a disk of plywood or MDF that can be firmly attached to a standard metal faceplate mounted on the headstock of the lathe. Many different work-holding fixtures can be constructed on false faceplates. For this project, the false faceplate needs to trap a square composed of 14 square sticks of wood. They're to be turned on one side, removed, rotated 180°, and turned on the other side.

In this situation the plywood faceplate should be larger than the square to be turned. Center the strips on the circle and take note of the center using a nail. Place brackets on all four sides and secure firmly.

I use bolts to hold it all together. It could be done by using an angle bracket and then screwing the parts together, but the bolts are the less risky way forward. Turned carefully there is not a lot of stress on the strips, but if they do start to move around the turning will be wrecked and it could fly off the lathe. Every caution must be taken.

Jigging. Bolt work-holding brackets onto a plywood disk.

Safety. Bolts are less risky than screws.

On Fragmented Turnings

This sequence of images shows the first thing to do after cutting up a newly turned form: play with the pieces. What are the possibilities? This kind of questioning can sidetrack the project, lead to confusion, and move the due date back, so it needs a certain care and resolve. Stick to the program most of the time, using the camera and sketchbook to record what you see and where things could go in the future. These playful mental and sometimes physical exercises are terribly important to the creative process.

The craft of turning was typically seen as a finished object coming off the lathe. However, if the turning is cut in half it may be put back together in a new way.

There is a vocabulary to the idea of fragments. Fundamentally it is about the simple geometry of cutting an object up. When something is cut in two it may then be put back more or less the same, in its original form. It may also be put back together differently. We do it all the time by cutting the tree down, planking it, selecting the piece from the board, and cutting it into ever-smaller pieces. One cut or multiple cuts will create quite different results. It's terribly simple really: halves, quarters, eighths, and so on.

The second idea to appreciate is words that activate, such as change, shift, flip, slide, turn, rotate, alternate, and so on. These are action words that suggest ways of seeing and working. This helps generate ideas about relationships within the parts. After cutting a piece apart, apply these words to the fragments. How might they reconnect? At first it may be best to not have a function in mind. The exercise is to come up with as many alternative configurations as possible. Some people may think of the results as sculpture, but more often I see it as investigations of form and construction.

The third idea is to evaluate the fragments from different criteria. What might they become? Is it functional, aesthetic, economic, or does it just remain an exercise for the mind? It does not have to have an immediate purpose. Sometimes useless things have a way of being unexpectedly engaging; you might say, "Wow, I never saw something like that before." To evaluate is to find the value in what you are looking at, and while you may be searching for one thing the unexpected may suggest something else. Being open to new possibilities does require an open attitude to new values.

The fourth idea is to always look for new relationships outside the work. It is comfortable to go with what is known, and tradition has value. It's been tested and found to work, so there is good reason to follow along. There is only so much new that may be brought to any project, so for starters go one step at a time—the best science experiments change only one thing at a time. Comparisons are equally essential in culture. We are building on what went before, whether it's building on the ideas of others or on ideas of your own. Considering relationships may also include bringing other objects or forms to the turning. Assembling disparate shapes, objects, and functions may bring about a new purpose. With these possibilities and relationships, the context of the turning evolves and is changed.

Vocabulary of fragments. The bird table from 1976 shows another way of cutting into the turned disk, and another way of seeing the fragments. Also see page 71.

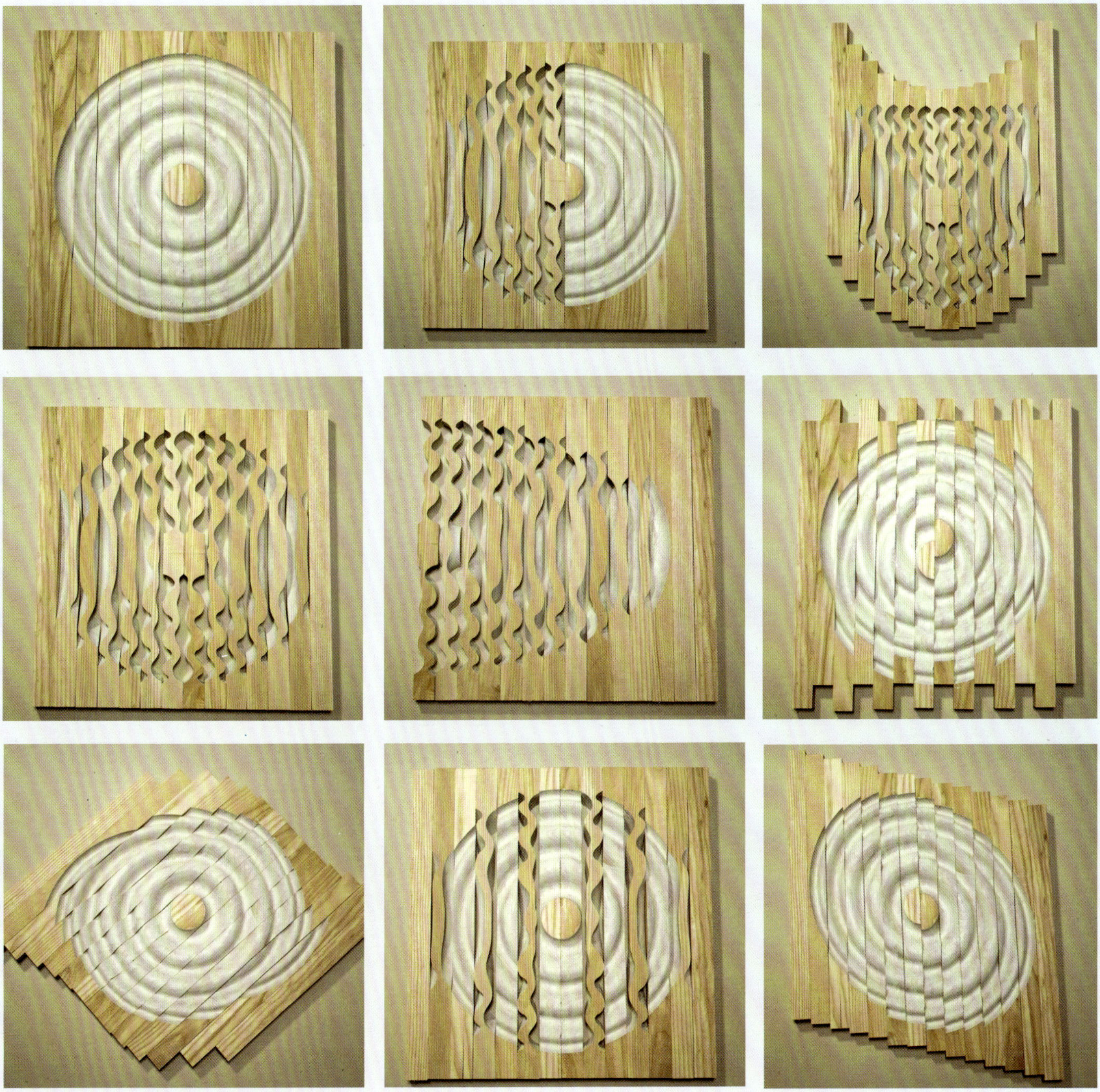

The camera records a few new possibilities.

Changing the Scale

On completion of any work it is important to pause and evaluate what happened. Think about making the same object in another material, and of increasing its scale. The path may be hidden in the work, the path may be just technical, functional, and physical, but it also can be emotional, spiritual, and intellectual. Use lenses like these to think about the work.

Made for an art gallery in London, Ontario, this screen exploits the turned cross section to good visual effect.

Library screen

In 1976, the architect Raymond Moriyama saw my small screen in an exhibition and asked if I could make one longer, maybe 200 feet long, to fence in the main reading room at the then-new downtown branch of the Toronto Library. I thought it possible, but I had to devise a new approach to achieve it (page 117). All projects have a potential to become more than originally intended.

COLLECTION: CITY OF TORONTO.

Library screen, 1977.
Red oak, concrete,
206′ long x 7′ high.

COLLECTION: MINISTRY OF GOVERNMENT SERVICES, ONTARIO.

Binary Spirit, installation, 1979. Black walnut, white pine, paint.

Binary Spirit, maquette, 1979. Black walnut, white pine, paint.

Wonder

Binary Spirit captures the idea of wonder. The photo above is of the model for the installation in Queens Park, Toronto. A large turned plate cut into strips makes the two halves, the evolving turning evokes the carved birds emerging in full flight. The subject is about turning and carving, equally shared with the evolving birds presented as a binary opposite of light and dark, art or craft. Asking either-or questions makes a weak relationship; rather, the question needs to expand: is it art, craft, design, or science? For me they are inseparable; every project contains all four aspects, but there may well be an emphasis in any given project.

CHAPTER 7

Spindle turning, cut apart

Towel Rack

Turning solves an everyday problem

Household needs are endless. The household need behind this project was for simple racks to dry towels and wet clothing in the bathroom and kitchen. I made two of them, and I'll detail both here to illustrate the process of design. For me, there is no doubt it gets better the second time around. After I made the first one, the industrial designer in me was alarmed by how many parts there were in the design, if it was made for production; I would need to simplify. The first towel rack is installed in the bathroom and works well there, but it does not quite celebrate the everyday, so I decided to make another using colored bobbins. Also, I wanted to sort out the drilling of the bobbins.

Sometimes household projects like this are a chore and at other times it is a nice challenge to make something charming, a delight to use, and better than most things on the market. My home is full of experiments and tried-out projects. Sometimes they go to market and sometimes it is for the pleasure of designing my own solution to an everyday problem. The dustpan I made in 1975 from the rear fender of a Karmann Ghia, shown on page 79, was an early example. While I could probably have picked up something from the dollar store, there is an intense pleasure from making one's own stuff even if it's a $100 solution rather than a $1 one.

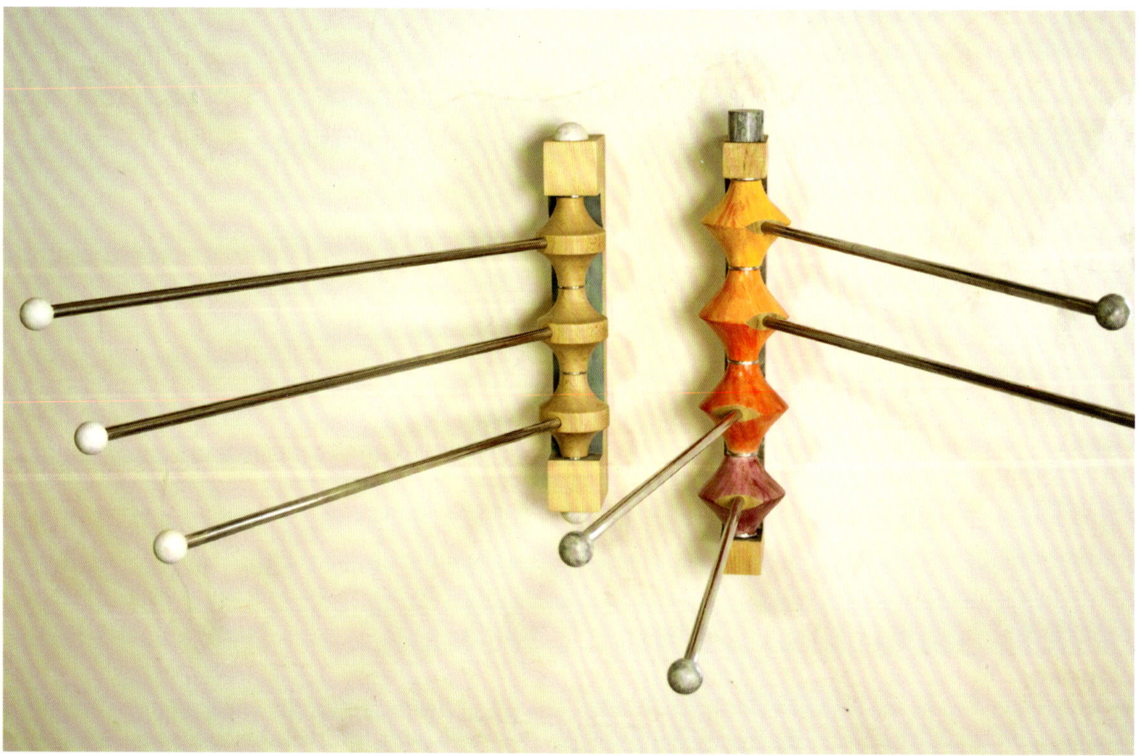

Designs get better the second time around. The first design, left, proves the concept and shines a light on the problems. The second design, right, solves some of them.

PHOTO BY MICHAEL MCLUHAN

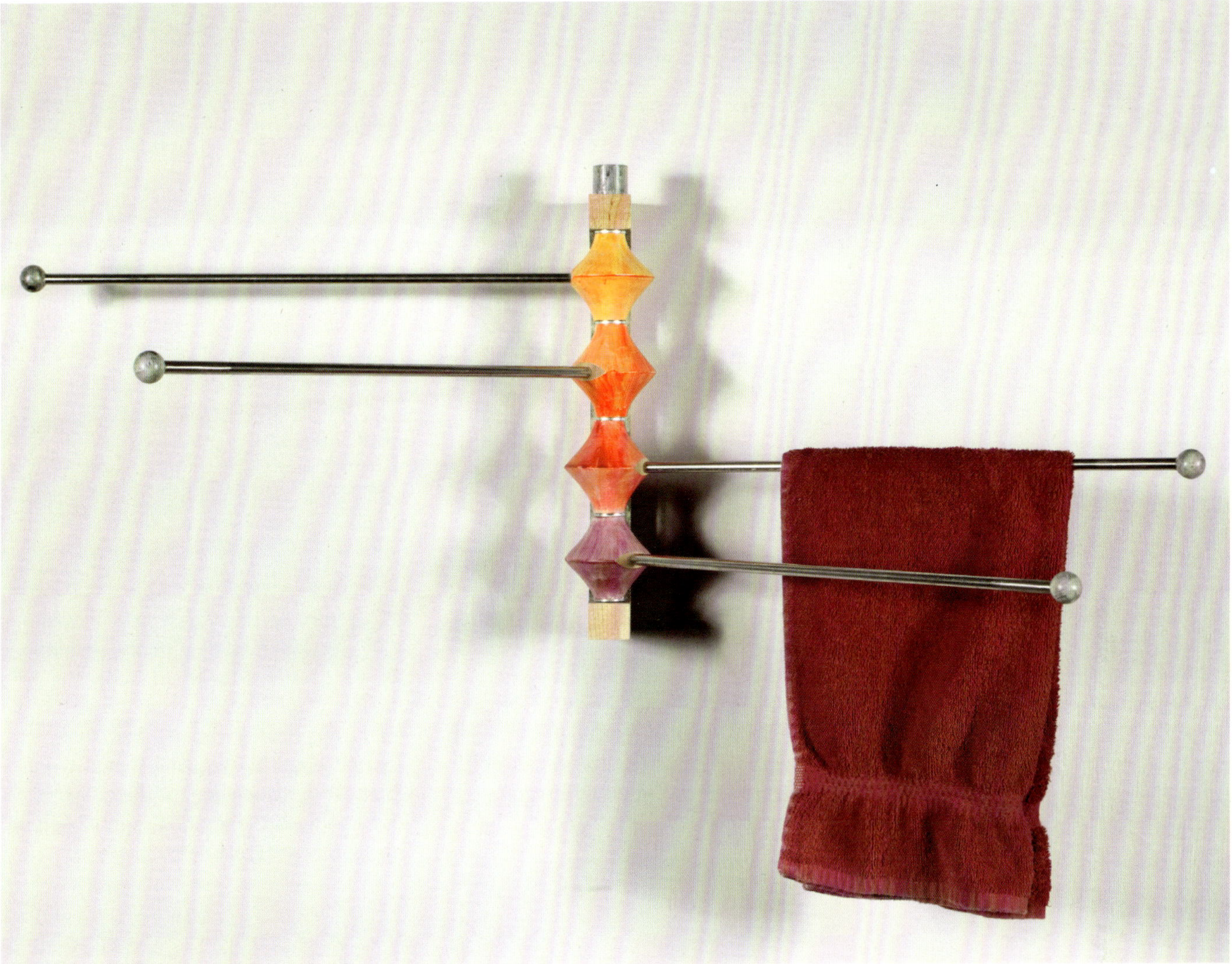

Towel Rack, 2012. Maple, steel rod, 12" (305mm) high.

> "It is a nice challenge to make something charming, a delight to use, and better than most things on the market."

Designing the towel rack

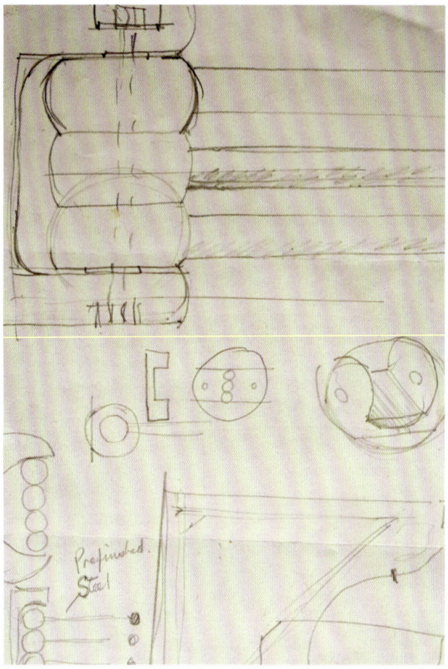

1 **Sketches.** Daily living made the need apparent for a substantial drying rack. The design started on a scrap piece of paper as a chunky series of turnings. Really ugly!

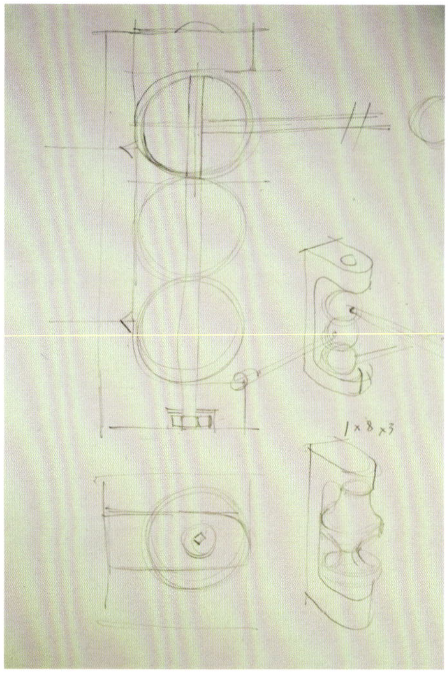

2 **Wood** spheres. After deciding to get serious, I developed more drawings in the sketchbook. Initially I was interested in purchasing wood spheres or balls from the hardware store, making this a turning project, but not one of my own making. Alas, I could not find the right-sized wooden ball.

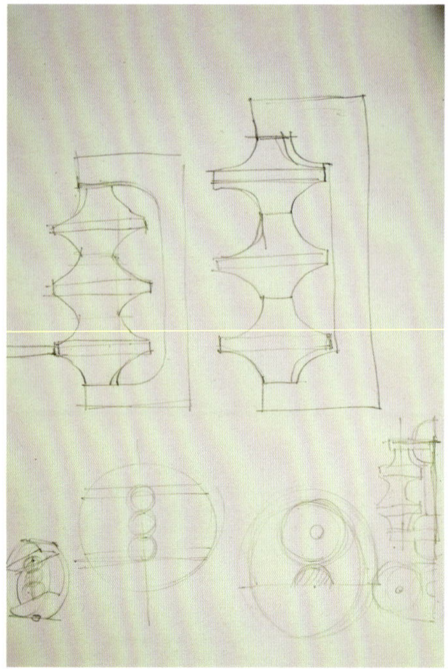

3 **Structure.** How much pressure could wet clothes on a 5⁄16" (8mm) stainless steel rod exert on the wood shape? The bobbin shape relates to the outward thrust of the rod. How much weight will there be on the wall bracket? Short-grain might break at the corner and the sketch shows two solutions. The one on the right beefs up the corner and looks better.

Turning and drilling

4 **Strength.** I chose to turn the bobbins from hard maple. The pressure on the arms from wet towels would be too much for a softwood and the bobbins would need to double in size.

5 **Cut and drill.** After turning I cut the bobbins apart with a handsaw, then drilled each one through the center for the 3⁄8" (9.5mm) threaded rod that would connect them to the bracket.

6 **Measure.** Before drilling for the arms, assemble the bobbins onto the threaded rod and measure the length, including steel washers, between the bobbins if you like that detail. A brad-point drill is best; use a depth gauge.

Making the bracket

7 **Extra wood.** Saw the back bracket from a hard maple block and clean it up with a mill file. The space for the bobbins must be accurate, allowing not only for the wood but also for the washers. This design has extra wood where short grain might snap.

8 **Trial assembly.** Now you can assemble the parts for the first time, and study the proportions again. How big should the back block be? Should it be narrower to emphasize the bobbins by having them project out further?

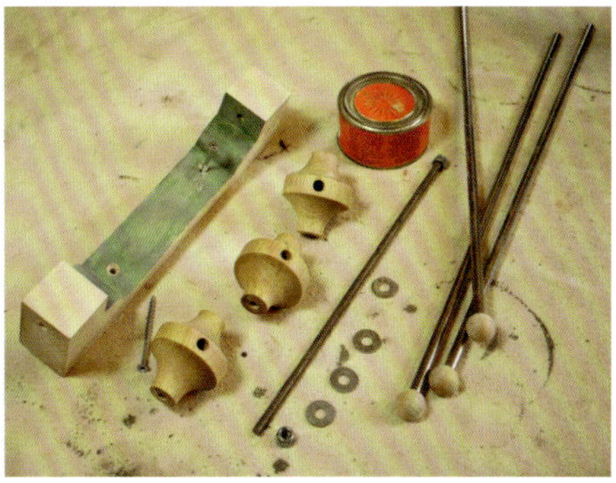

9 **Finishing.** Paint the parts as a backdrop for the bobbins. Finish the natural wood with urethane varnish and wax the metal before assembly.

Turning the second rack

10 **Drill first.** For the second drying rack, I used the self-centering chuck to mount a turning blank of pear wood from the tree that had been stripped by the porcupine (page 26). I drilled ⅜" in diameter from one end and then the other; the holes almost met and with a little help from the long twist bit everything lined up.

11 **Big forces.** The bobbins may be any length; the critical dimension is the diameter. The stainless steel 5⁄16" (8mm) arm will be drilled into the thickest section, and imagine someone grabbing hold of that to help stand up. It's quite a force that is not in the job description, but it is what people do to your designs.

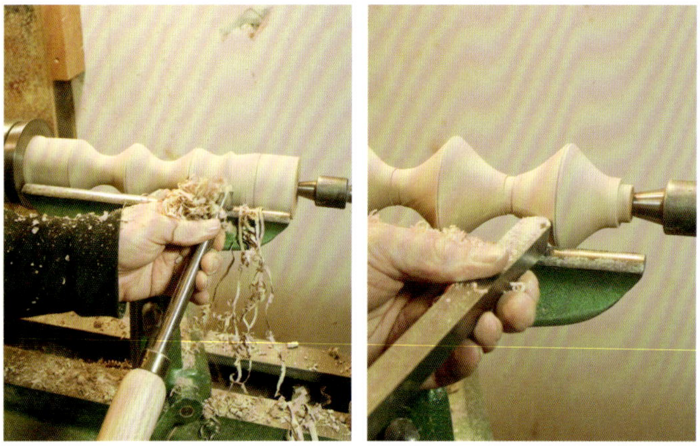

12 Turning. I used a gouge to rough the shapes out (left) and I usually finish with a scraper (right), though I know a production turner would get a perfect surface from the skew chisel.

13 Part off. The parting tool marks precisely where the bobbins will be sanded to a clean crisp edge before they get cut off.

14 Finishing. This time I finished the bobbins on the lathe, first with an undercoat and then some filler on a tiny knot. Sand lightly, then apply another undercoat.

Drilling the bobbins

15 Preparation. Make a flat on each bobbin where you will drill for the rod. The belt sander is aggressive and you may prefer to use a regular bastard file and then finish on abrasives glued to a board. The flat on the turned bobbin makes a really wonderful shape ready for drilling.

16 Jigging. Mark out with an awl where the brad-point bit will drill for the arm. It's good to have the bobbins in a vee-block jig so the drilling is square in one direction and the turning can't roll around.

17 Small details. The small level resting on the right-hand flat helps get the other direction square. To make household items that really do work well, it's important to put attention on small details like this.

Assembly and painting

18 **Separate bobbins.** The vee-block jig continues to hold the turning while I saw off the bobbins. You can use a hand saw or the band saw for this job.

19 **Trial assembly.** Number the parts and keep the order in your first trial assembly. I had to remove ⅛" (3mm) from the support block to get it all to fit.

20 **Cap the rod.** The ⅜" (10mm) threaded rod needs a cap for the top and possibly the bottom. The top cap is essential or the rod could drop through. I cut off a dowel and drilled it to receive a nut glued in with epoxy.

21 **Colors.** Paint the bobbins with colors you like. I chose a palette of analogous colors all based on red but sliding towards yellow/red in one direction and blue/red in the other.

22 **End caps.** I decided to add small wooden balls on the ends of the rods to protect a person who might back into the drying rack after a bath or shower. The balls were painted a mid-gray.

23 **Varnish.** I prefer to apply the paints as a thin wash, followed by a protective coat of polyurethane varnish. A spray can of varnish does a good job on small objects.

Household Needs

Beginnings

This was the first piece I made during my 1975 residency at Melbourne State College, and an early attempt to make something useful by cutting into a disk turned on the faceplate. It was designed during the 20-hour airplane flight from Canada to Australia. Eggs are about beginnings and breakfast is about breaking the fast and also about breaking into the egg shell. Silky oak was new to me, along with all the tools and equipment at the college. There is something special about the start of something new and that is what each day should bring to the work. For me all these experiences and ideas flow through the piece.

COLLECTION: AUSTRALIAN COUNCIL FOR THE ARTS, CRAFTS BOARD.
PHOTO BY TONY BOYD

Egg Cup, 1975. Silky brown oak, 4.5" (114mm) x 8.25" (210mm) x 2" (51mm).

Commonplace

As I wrote in my first book, *Wood Turning: The Purpose of the Object*, I made this piece for a student named Avo, after the handle had broken on his potato masher. Avo really likes mashed potatoes. We discussed the mashing action, the shape of the metal, the feel of the handle, the thrust and twist of the potato-mashing art. The commonplace need not be common, obvious, or meaningless. Rather, everyday is a place where we may all meet on the commons. I hope Avo still enjoys his mashed potatoes and the masher.

PHOTO BY TONY BOYD COLLECTION: AVO, AUSTRALIA.

Potato masher, 1975. Eucalyptus mallee root, 8.5" (216mm) x 3.5" (89mm).

Re-use, Repair, Recycle

The dust pan (right) was made soon after I returned to Canada after a year of teaching in Australia. I was in a new studio workshop and needed to get the most basic things together. The dust pan was not a quick solution because the pan had to be cut from the fender of a Volkswagen Karmann Ghia just before it went to the wrecking yard. Where the handle attaches is where the rear lights would have been. A really interesting dust pan should make more pleasurable the everyday activity of sweeping up. There is a correlation between good tools and good work. For me it also is an early example of the 3 Rs: Re-Use, Repair and Recycle, although any culture in the past would have been involved in making things work again rather than just throwing them out as we do.

COLLECTION: THE ARTIST.

Karmann Ghia Dust Pan, 1975. Various woods, 26" (660mm) x 15" (381mm) x 6" (152mm).

Tough wood

Bull oak (below) is a very tough wood typical of Australian trees growing in arid conditions. The color is majestic, a sort of crushed cardinal that darkens over time, a bit like dried blood. Typical of oak, the ray cells are dramatic. It's a wood for turners, though tough on sharp chisels, and not much good to cabinet makers.

COLLECTION: THE ARTIST.

Knife Rack, 1975.
Bull oak, epoxy filler,
13.5" (343mm) x
6" (152mm) dia.

Presentation

My daughter Rebecca needs to present photographic albums for scrapbooking. The stand was made from the base for a side table, a large turning in basswood cut and painted. It has a presence from either side. The book is small and the albums will just about cover the 16" x 20" (406 x 508mm) panel; the shelf support measures 28" long. This design moves towards a lectern without legs or a dictionary stand to rest on a table.

COLLECTION: REBECCA RAINSFORD.

Album Display, 2011. Ash, basswood, 28" wide.

Fits the book

The dimensions of a book stand relate to the size of book to be presented. This wall-mounted project was made specifically to hold *The Joy of Cooking* or Julia Childs' *The Way to Cook*, my partner's most-used cookbooks. The turned element that supports the book was left over from drawer handles on another project.

Neapolitan Book Stand, 2011. Various hardwoods, 20" wide.

Drawer pull

A fragment sawn from a long spindle can make an attractive and useful handle for doors and drawers. This example was made for the kitchen of a friend, and there is a similar one in our own kitchen at home. The shape is like the curving brackets we use to draw together several related points. It's an elegant shape that pulls everything together even as it opens the cabinet.

Bracketing Drawer Handle. Ash, paint, varying lengths.

CHAPTER 8

Spindle and faceplate turnings

Four Walking Canes

Carved, turned, turned-and-carved, found in the woods

In February, on a sheet of black ice with a dusting of white powdered snow, my partner Margaret fell and broke an ankle. After two operations to reset the bones, she was in a wheelchair for a few months, but eventually she would need a walking cane. This would be my second walking stick for Margaret, the first having been lost from the top of a car after a quick getaway. On this occasion I made three: one carved, one turned, and one turned and carved. The first had an ergonomic handle carved to fit the patient's hand. While carving the handle I got the idea for a second design that might work as a production model featuring two turnings. The third was a grander solution more complicated to make, with three turnings and some carving—a shepherd's crook. Alongside these increasingly detailed solutions, I had a fourth stick of my own for walking in the woods, cut to length with nothing added.

The initial concept for Margaret's cane was based on a saddle supporting the handle, the inverse of a person riding a horse. It's a structural idea and not the typical way of making a walking cane. It worked well except for the choice of wood. The shaft was ash with an apple handle, and while the color of the apple was a wonderful contrast, it shrank ⅛" (3mm) from 1" (25mm), leaving a gap to be filled and me shuddering every time I see it. The apple came from the firewood pile and after two years it had not dried that well. The shaft and handle were glued with 24-hour epoxy but even then it pulled apart, though it did remain strong with just the one side connecting. The cane could not be thrown away as it was essential to getting around and I had many pressures from other projects. Although I did ultimately complete all four canes, the first one, which had traveled to New York and helped Margaret around the Museum of Modern Art, Metropolitan Museum of Art, and Natural History Museum, remained her favorite. It's not often my work gets around like that!

"The saddle supporting the handle is a structural idea and not the typical way of making a walking cane."

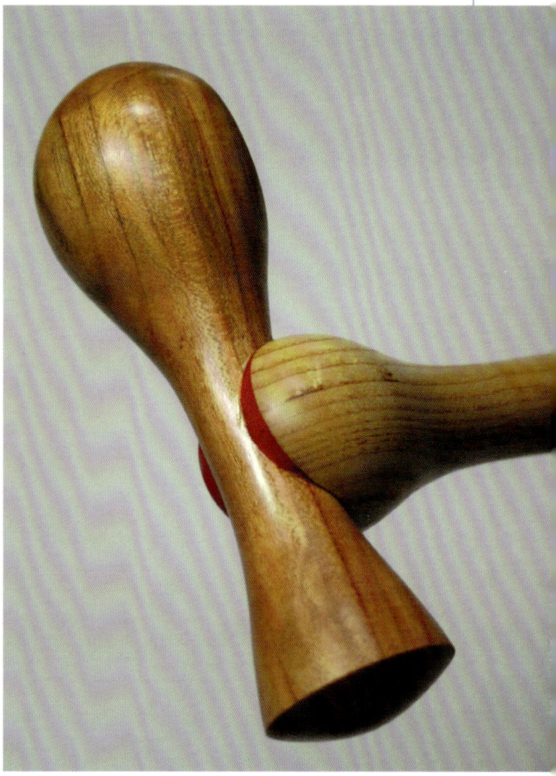

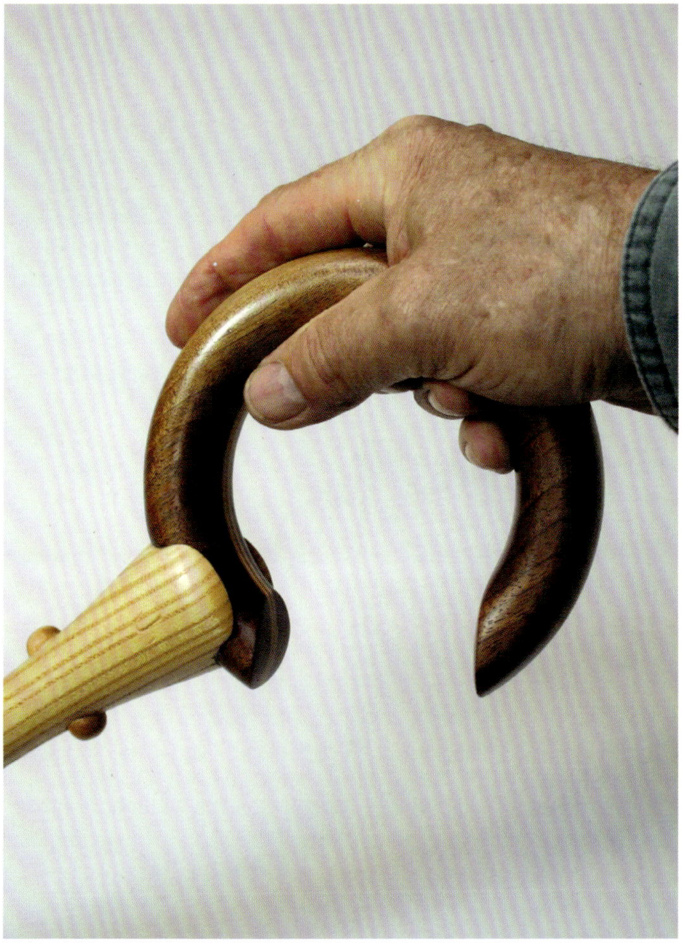

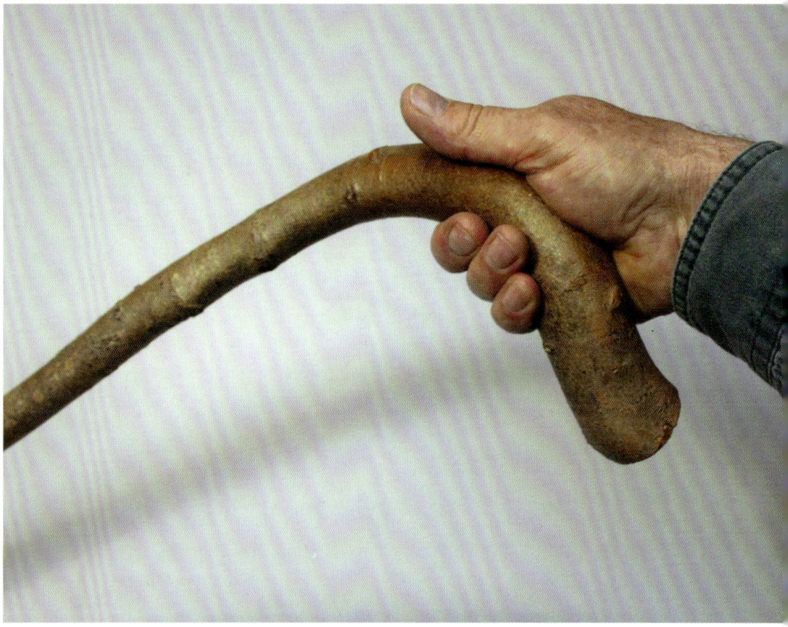

Four canes, 2012. The rustic cane that I found in the woods is in the last photo. Clockwise, the carved cane, turned cane, rustic cane, and turned-and-carved cane.

First cane: carved

1 **Design.** The drawing for the first cane happened quickly without the agonizing that comes with some designs. The handle would be turned and then carved to fit the hand.

2 **Wood.** The 2" x 2" x 34" (51 x 51 x 864mm) blank came from an ash staircase off-cut. Ash wood is springy with long fibers so breaking it is difficult. The handle, rust-colored fine-grained apple from the firewood pile, had been stacked for a couple of years and felt dry. But apple is liable to be unstable.

Turning the shaft

3 **Bulb for joint.** After roughing out the blank, I made the bulb for the handle first. At this point it is too large, but refinement will follow later.

4 **Foot fits tip.** At the other end of the shaft I turned the foot down to its final size, to fit the inside diameter of the rubber tip.

5 **Joint design.** The bulb needed some on-the-turning design work to establish the dimensions of the handle. The generous 2" (51mm) diameter eventually came down to 1⅞" (48mm). The saddle drawn on the turning shows how much wood will be left after inserting the 1" (25mm) wide handle.

"The first cane has an ergonomic handle carved to fit the patient's hand."

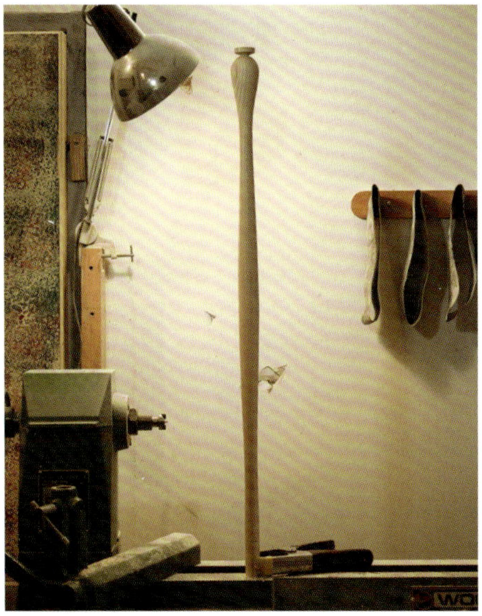

6 **Refine shapes.** Now it's possible to refine the shapes by taking the turning off the lathe and standing it up the way it will be seen. The flow of lines is critical, as is keeping enough material for strength. Finding the compromise takes time.

Fitting the handle

7 **Jigging.** The vee-jig cradles the workpiece while drilling out space for the handle. This saddle shape could have been cut as a square, but making it round brings consistency with all the other curves in the project.

8 **Saw waste.** Mark out where to cut the slot for the handle and then remove the waste with a small hand saw.

9 **Carve.** The apple block was sawn to fit, then filed to be really snug. Next I carved its shape, looking for an ergonomic fit of wood to hand. Frequent discussion and trial fittings produced a surprisingly ugly shape pleasing to the hand but not the eye.

10 **Glue.** The carved handle was glued to the shaft using two-part epoxy and very gentle clamping, being careful not to squeeze all the glue out of the joint. Optimistically I hoped the apple wood was now stable and the epoxy would hold things together.

11 **Clean up.** After the epoxy had set, I clamped the assembled cane to the workbench for final clean-up of the joint and grip.

12 **Wriggle factor.** The bulb holding the handle was a little too big and had to be carved some more. The shape caused the fingers to bunch up without any wriggle factor, that is, the ergonomic need for the body to keep moving around.

Second cane: turned production

13 **Minimal carving.** While carving the handle I formed the idea for a production model that would be quicker to make. The principle is simple: two turnings with minimal carving.

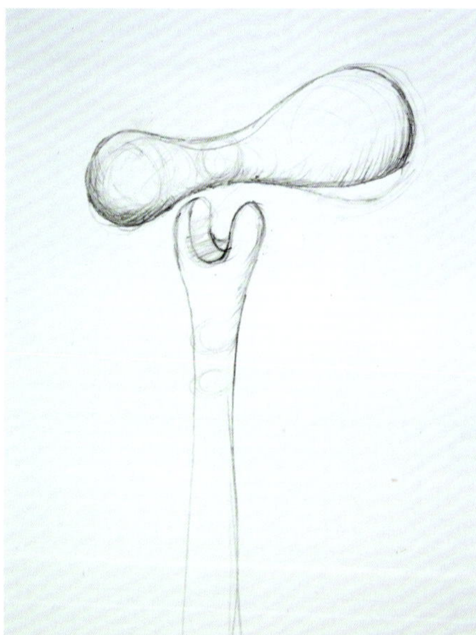

14 **Compare.** I turned another shaft and compared the two. I always like to have more than one sketch and, if possible, more than one turned shape. The comparison suggested making the new one slimmer and more elegant with a smaller bulb for small hands. The curve of the shaft feels more buoyant and alive.

15 **Turn to fit.** To simplify fitting, I drilled the cane at the bulb and turned the handle to the same diameter.

16 **Snug.** The turned handle fits the shaft satisfyingly snugly.

Glue and clamp

17 **Wax resist.** Before gluing with two-part epoxy, I applied wax on areas where I didn't want the glue absorbing into the wood.

18 **Glue sets.** Clamp the assembly overnight so the epoxy can fully cure.

19 **Fill gaps.** The design detail called for colored epoxy to fill the gaps at the top of the handle. Highlighting the connection adds some life.

Third cane: turned-and-carved

20 **Design.** I liked the crook-handled form (see Design Evolution) but needed to determine how to make it support a heavy person putting all their weight on the cane. Too much snap-able short grain needed reinforcement. I used ¼" (6mm) Baltic birch plywood as a structural spine connecting handle to shaft.

21 **Layers.** I chose contrasting walnut to go on each side of the plywood to form the structural sandwich, and used double-sided tape to mount the walnut on a false faceplate. It's a simple turning with the cross section of a semicircle, but you do need to turn two that match.

22 **Saw spine.** Cut out the plywood spine with a coping saw or a jig saw.

23 **Oversize.** The plywood should be 1⁄16" (2mm) bigger than the turnings, so that after glue-up the assembly can be filed down smooth.

24 **Fitting.** Figuring out how to fit all the parts together took some care, and developing the saddle in the shaft was difficult. I used the wire pattern-copying device; it's not very accurate but does indicate what's going on.

Fitting the handle

25 **Glue handle.** I decided to glue the handle parts together to settle their relationship. Fitting more than two parts at once can lead to chaos; however, to move ahead all three parts had to go together and be filed to their final smooth surface.

26 **Saw the saddle.** Draw the profile of the handle on the shaft, then rough out the saddle with a band saw or coping saw. Clean up using rat-tail files or, if you want to live dangerously, a drum sander. When the handle profile fits into the shaft, mark out the exact placement of the structural plywood.

27 **Fit the parts.** Saw the slot in the shaft of the cane, ease the plywood membrane down into the slot, and fit the handle into the saddle. It's difficult to see but there is a flat on the handle that connects onto another flat in the saddle.

28 **Glue.** Two-part epoxy glues the parts together. A little black acrylic powder makes the glue darker. I like the dark glue line as the wood ages, also getting darker.

29 **File and sand.** Clean up the plywood spine of the handle where it enters the shaft. File the wood into rough shape, then refine with strips of old sanding belt. Go through the grits to 150 before you switch to sanding with the grain.

30 **Saw crook.** With the shaft completed, band-saw out the handle to make the crook. File and sand the ends smooth. Notice the projecting button added where the plywood spine joins the shaft of the cane. The round hole is less likely than a square mortise to split. It also looks great!

Design Evolution

Designs evolve. I made the first cane to fit my partner's hand. It worked but was not too attractive and was tedious to make. That gave rise to the second design, a production cane assembled from two simple turnings.

While working on the first two walking canes I searched for different designs. The traditional crook-handle cane seemed like a challenge for a turner. So I developed a turned crook-handle cane using some of the things I had learned from the first canes. The drawings show how the designs evolved.

The saddle connection was a design idea from 1959 when I was a student, I remember an instructor saying the ideas worked on at school will probably keep repeating. More than fifty years later this seems to be true, except I often find the idea has matured. I was also told that people in the visual arts just get better as they get older, unlike dancers who have a limited career due to the physical rigors of the discipline. There is as always the risk that we'll slip on ice and break a leg when we're older, and wood has a way of taking charge and shrinking when not expected. We have to remain students of nature.

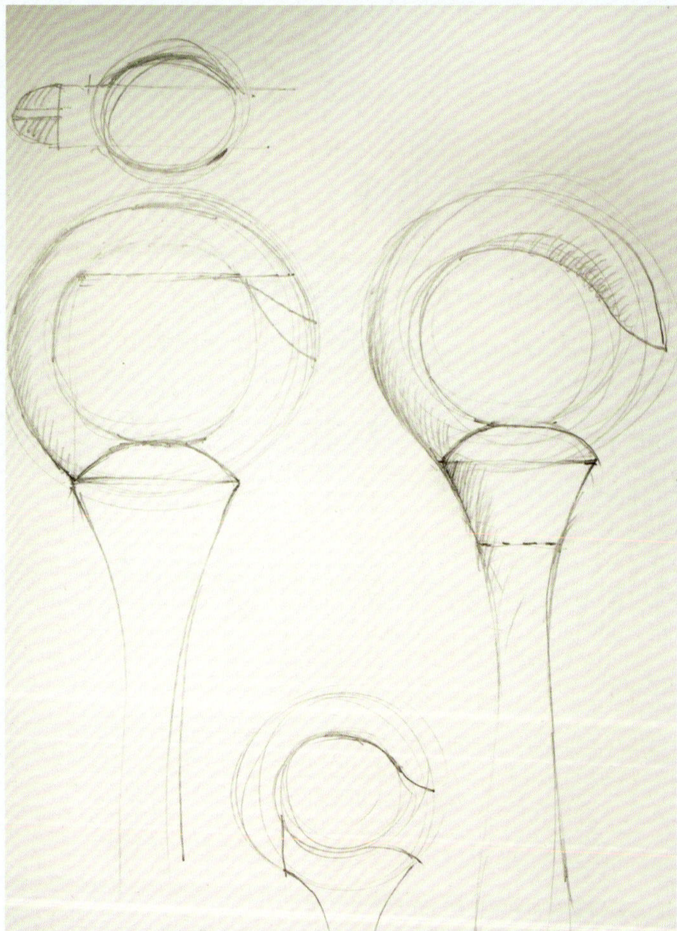

Second sketch teases out the shepherd's crook.

First sketch establishes the idea and basic dimensions.

Fourth Cane: Found in the Woods

At the end of the project I went into the bush to look for more examples of the grown handle. The first would be about the right dimension with the bark removed. The second is too big but full of potential for a carved solution. The third tree is growing in a most unusual configuration that stimulates new ways of thinking about a handle. It's been a bit roughed up by the foresters hauling logs but still would be my first choice. It will not mature to be a sound tree and so would be usefully thinned.

A final thought: when in the country make sure you have permission to cut trees. I have some really unusually shaped trees and would be very annoyed if someone cut them down to make a walking stick or firewood. Trees have wonderful forms and I like to enjoy them in their place.

Big enough to carve.

About the right size.

Something new here.

CHAPTER 9

Faceplate turning, cut and rejoined

The Walking Bowl

Expressive form is tricky to make

Technically the walking bowl is not too complex to make, but people often cannot sort out how it possibly could have been turned on the lathe. It's simply a shape like an airplane propeller with a small bowl turned in its middle. Then it's cut in half and the two pieces joined rim to rim so the propeller blades now become legs that support the reconstituted bowl. While the necessary fragments could be sawn from a disk, much of the disk would be discarded and it would hardly be economical of material. Instead, I begin by sawing a thick plank of wood into thin wings extending from a thick central block. The blank then gets mounted on the faceplate with a supporting disk of plywood, which keeps it from being an actual airplane propeller bearing down on my fingers.

Many turners use this approach to create complex objects on multiple centers. By building work-holding fixtures onto a faceplate, you can turn the surfaces of a balanced blank that contains the fragments of interest for your project. This is true for every size of lathe. I often work at a large scale, turning elements for staircase installations and large public sculpture (see Milling Machine, page 117). But you can explore these same ideas at whatever scale your lathe can handle. The principles are the same, and so are the technical requirements.

The maple used for this demonstration project was cut down in 2003 by the local electric utility to clear power lines; then I used a chain-saw to cut a slab approximately 4½" (114mm) thick. The wood was put into a shed and left until about four years ago, when it was brought inside. There is something very satisfying about a large slab of rough wood and as I started to measure it for a walking bowl it occurred to me to retain some of this rough, gutsy quality. The walking bowl has usually been a more refined object but in this demonstration I wanted to bring together these different qualities. Living in the country, it is easier to enjoy what some refer to as rusticity compared to the sophistications of urbanity. Actually, I think sophistication occurs in the appropriate application of different qualities. Sometimes I drink beer and, other times, champagne.

Usually I will make three of these bowls at one time. Each setup enables three and the third is exponentially faster. When one piece has been glued or set aside for the finish to dry, it's possible to work on the others. Also, making decisions about the design is more relaxed because I can compare the three pieces. There is something to be said for production, though, for me, within limits!

> "People often cannot sort out how it possibly could have been turned on the lathe."

Walking Bowl, 2012. Maple, paint, 16" (405mm) tall.

Walking Bowl Proportions and Scale

The proportions of a walking bowl are important to get right. Over the years I have experimented with many variations and what works best for me is a cross section close to 4" (102mm) thick and 8" (203mm) wide. A blank 3" (76mm) thick and 6" (152mm) wide has the same proportions; 2" (51mm) thick by 4" (102mm) wide will make a very small bowl. Long legs make for elegance but can be unstable, while short legs are more stable and functional to use.

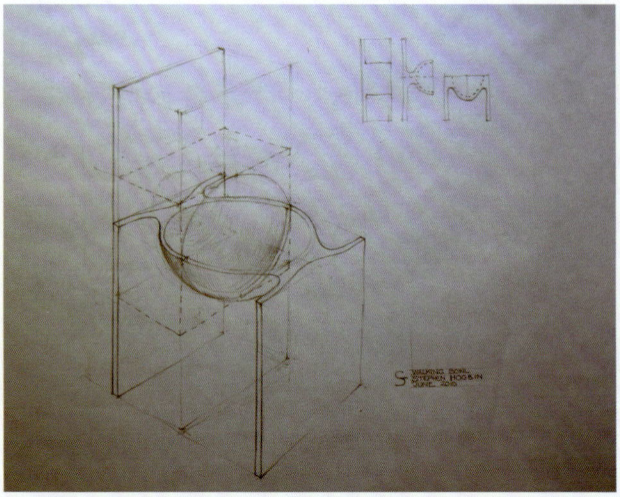

Walking Bowl

Prepare the blank

1 **Wood blank.** Begin by flattening one face of the rough-sawn billet, using a portable power plane or hand planes, then put it through the thickness planer and bring it to the maximum thickness, in this instance a generous 4" (102mm).

2 **Make two.** Since I planned to make three walking bowls, I cut the 60" (1524mm) plank into two 18" (457mm) slabs and one 24" (610mm) slab.

3 **Square corner.** With a face side established, next make an accurate face-edge. One square corner is essential. Tack a straight strip of wood to one edge so the band saw has a line to follow, then plane the sawn face-edge smooth and flat.

"The supporting disk of plywood keeps it from being an airplane propeller bearing down on my fingers."

Mark out

4 **Find center.** Locate and mark out the center of the blank and draw a circle to define the bowl form that will be turned there.

5 **Saw with care.** Band-saw the legs to about ⅜" (10mm) thick, and take care not to over-cut the line; I usually finish with a hand saw. The green masking tape helps establish a straight sawing line on the rough wood.

6 **Wall thickness.** Find the center and determine the wall thickness of the bowl. When there is a wane edge involved, this can be a bit trickier than with a fully squared block.

7 **No corners.** Saw the corners using the table saw or a hand saw, then break this waste away from the blank.

Mount

8 **Support.** Glue a plywood disk to support the faceplate onto the leg side of the block. Plywood is easier than hardwood to take off after the turning. Depending on the size of your lathe, you may need to mount the faceplate outboard.

9 **Safety.** The walking bowl is like an airplane propeller on the lathe and with contact, serious body damage will occur. Loose clothing also could get snagged. Therefore, use double-sided tape to attach a safety disk of thin plywood so it spans the full length of the blades.

10 **Center hole.** The plywood safety disk has a center hole for the plywood block where the faceplate mounts.

11 **Mount outboard.** The completed faceplate assembly was too large to fit inboard on my lathe so it had to be mounted outboard.

Turn

12 **Safety.** With the lathe switched on, the legs become a dangerous blur. The plywood safety disk is not optional, but essential.

13 **Outside first.** Turn the outside of the bowl first, taking extreme care not to cut into the flat plane of the legs. A scraping chisel works best for me because it is less inclined to catch.

14 **Transition.** The cut that makes the transition from the bowl into the leg is particularly tricky. Keep the tool rest in close to help you avoid a catch, which could rip the chisel out of your hands. Sand the outside to 180 grit now.

15 **Inside.** Turn out the inside of the bowl, working from the lip or edge to the center. Establish the final wall thickness at the start and stick with it as the bowl progresses. I find a ¼" (6mm) wall to be a good thickness for gluing the bowl together later.

16 **Caliper walls.** Check the wall thickness with calipers. I usually develop a smooth form but curved or wavy lines might also work, though building too many ideas in one piece will probably confuse the viewer.

Smooth

17 **Demount.** Remove the piece from the lathe and unscrew the faceplate. The plywood mounting block needs to be whacked off with a broad chisel or cut off with a hand saw.

18 **Plane the legs.** Smooth the legs on either side of the bowl. Hand planes work well for me, though the plane can get only so close before it bangs into the bowl and damages it.

19 **Sanding.** The palm sander completes the job, in this instance starting with 100 grit and working up to 220 grit.

20 **Defect.** One of the legs had a serious check from the end of the plank. I am unsure whether to round into the check or to fill it with colored epoxy (see Fixing Cracks, Checks, and Calamities). That's a decision to make later, when I know more about the nature of this bowl.

21 **Smooth transitions.** Drum sanders help make the transition from the roundness of turning to the flat plane of the leg.

"Hand-sanding completes the surface finish, a satisfying stage to reach."

22 **Hand sanding.** Finally, and what you probably don't want to hear, hand-sanding completes the surface finish. This is a satisfying stage to reach!

Cut apart

23 **Cut where?** Now where to cut the bowl? This is the fun part where the cross section is revealed. If the bowl is to carry a sense of movement then it must be cut on a diagonal. The amount of angle will get the bowl strolling or running. This time it's a slow subtle movement.

24 **Straight cut.** The band saw is the tool of choice for this straight cut, and there you have it, two halves to make a new whole.

25 **Remove wedge.** One cut is good but two is often better. Removing a small wedge shape helps to articulate the gesture, by opening the legs at the front and closing them at the back. Mark the same amount off each side, in this case about ½" (13mm) tapering to nothing.

26 **Curves.** This is the time to put a curve into the cross section. Always work to a drawn line. The shape may develop as you carve away material but the line helps you to not lose your way, especially when there are two identical sides. I'm using a die grinder; carving tools and rasps would also do.

"Always work to a drawn line as you carve; it helps you to not lose your way."

Fill checks

27 **Fill defects.** The end of this day is the time to fill the check with epoxy, so it can dry overnight. Mix up two-part epoxy with a touch of the colorant. Mix thoroughly and putty it into the gap, leaving it built up high to counteract with any shrinkage.

28 **Sand smooth.** After the epoxy has cured overnight, file it back to the wood surface and sand smooth. Be sure to wear a mask and avoid breathing any epoxy dust.

Rejoin

29 **Square edges.** Having made the wedge cut on the band saw and liking the amount the leg opens, take the workpieces to the disk sander and square their edges. Go slow because the sander tends to catch these shapes and leave a little chatter, or it might grab an edge and rip the workpiece out of your hands.

30 **Sand smooth.** Finish the edges on sandpaper mounted on a flat board. Hold the workpiece firmly and rub without rocking. Screeching indicates vibration and the surface will not be perfect—shift your grip and try again. Hold the two halves together and if you can see any light, sand some more.

31 **Rub joint.** Shapes like this one can be impossible to clamp, so I make a rub joint. Coat both surfaces with PVA glue, rub the mating surfaces together, and hold it in your hands with firm pressure for about two minutes. It helps if the room is warm—and don't use extended glue or you may be holding for two hours.

32 **Glue squeeze.** Stand the glued piece down gently so the joint is not stressed and support the high leg overnight so the glue can fully cure. The glue squeeze-out in the photo is about right; after a few hours it will be leather-hard and you can slice the bead off the wood.

33 **File smooth.** I use files to clean up the bottom or outside of the bowl and the connecting edge. The smooth mill file produces the best final finish.

34 **Sand inside.** The inside is tedious to clean up; usually a small disk sander will get in there to smooth the final alignment and create a perfect eggshell.

Oops

When you read books like this, you might get the erroneous impression that everything always goes right. It doesn't. While I try to see mistakes and mishaps as new opportunities for creative exploration, the plain truth is that sometimes you just have to grind and sand the blunder away. These two photos show a typical situation, resolved by patience and elbow grease.

Oops. The band-saw blade went in too deep when the block was first cut so there is quite a bit of carving to get the shape to work. The tool marks in this case are from the die grinder, which need to be cut back with abrasives.

Sand smooth. To remove the grinder marks, I took these longer abrasive tubes from the oscillating sander, cut a rod to fit inside, and powered them with the drill. Next, use the palm sander if it will fit, and if not, finish up by hand.

Finish

35 **Eggshell base.** Two generous undercoats, rubbed back with sandpaper in between, help conceal wonky alignment between the two halves of the bowl and also create the eggshell base for layers of color.

36 **Thin coats.** The colors were driven by the epoxy filler in the leg with the check. It turned out to be pink rather than red. I started by laying down several thin coats of yellow acrylic artists' paint.

37 Texture forms. Next I applied red-orange paint with a wet brush and you can see the texture forming. The paint runs and some parts dry quicker than others. I am careful not to get the raspberry jam look where it slides to the bottom of the bowl and forlornly puddles there.

38 More color. I cut back the red with 120-grit sandpaper and added some dabs of blue, which aligned the paint with the pink epoxy filler. It worked but still wasn't what I wanted so I dabbed on some pink polka dots to pull all the colors together.

Orienting the Grain

Thick planks of wood offer the turner a decision about grain patterns. If you orient the blank so the radial (quarter-sawn) surface is forward, it will show a refined pin-stripe quality, but the trade-off is likely to be the smaller size that can be sawn from the plank. However if you orient the blank so the tangential flat-sawn surface dominates, the bowl can be larger but the grain will be broader and less uniform. It depends on what you are making and the qualities you intend it to have.

For the walking bowl shown here, I chose the pin-stripe quartersawn figure because its scale works better with the elegance of the form. I also kept a bit of the waney edge, thinking it might be useful in the finished piece to reveal its essential treeness.

Dry wood. After drying since 2003, the maple is ready to use. But which way to orient the wood grain?

More Curves

The walking bowl shown in the main demonstration has straight and flat legs. That is the simplest approach. Sometimes, however, I want the legs to echo the curve of the bowl itself—they seem more animated that way. The curve can be a single sweep or it can be rippled like linen-fold carving, it depends on the gesture you intend to animate. If you want to try this, do the shaping before you turn the central bowl. Be careful when turning not to cut into the almost finished carved leg (see Oops, page 102).

Refine. With a complex form in wood, there's no escaping the slow process of refinement with drum sanders, orbital sanders, and hand-sanding through the grits.

Draw curves. Use a bent steel ruler to draw a dynamic curve on the end of the leg. In this piece I modified the curve to a linen-fold shape. It is as if the leg becomes fabric blowing freely.

Grind. Flip the piece over and shape what will become the inside of the leg. The die-grinder hogs off material quickly.

Carve. Remove the material using carving chisels, a die-grinder, or even the chain saw. Once roughed out I refine the form with rasps and files.

Transitions. Inevitably the transition from turning to leg is always tricky. Use a chisel and mallet, but be wary of the grain as one side will chip away nicely and the other will probably not.

Color Schemes and Textures

Painting the insides of cut and re-glued bowls helps hide the inevitable misalignment between the halves. Two generous layers of a white undercoat begins the process, with sanding in between to improve adhesion and create a smooth base.

Normally the color scheme begins with the color of the wood itself. I like to work with analogous colors that are next to one another on the color chart (see page 41). In the demonstration walking bowl shown here, the epoxy filler, which I had intended to be red, came out a bit salmon-pink due to the grey color of the epoxy itself. The wood is quite bland in color so I decided to continue with this pink hue inside the bowl.

I like to lay down transparent layers of color so they glimmer through subsequent coats. Experience told me that a base coat of yellow acrylic would be the best place to begin. I followed that with red-orange to match the epoxy, applied somewhat thick with a wet brush so it would leave a texture of brush marks. Take care not to allow the wet color to dribble or form puddles.

Once you have the base color you like, cut it back with 120-grit sandpaper. This creates a texture that the next coat of paint can cling to—some dabs of blue and then pink in the demonstration project—but more important, I am looking for interest in the texture. I'll encourage the paint to drip, crack, and form patterns in itself. That's because I am consciously wanting to avoid the uniform perfection of a mechanically applied industrial finish. The hand finish talks to the idea of a relaxed and perfect imperfection, a casual elegance. Machines can't imitate that.

Yellow

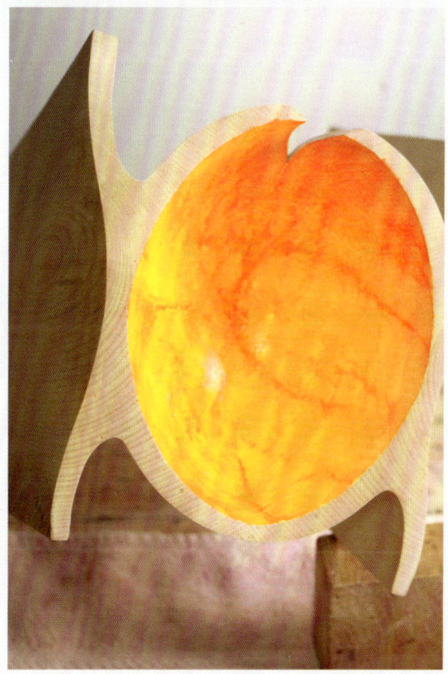

Red

Fixing Cracks, Checks, and Calamities

There are various ways to fix things when the wood has a mind of its own. The most common problem for turners is a check or crack in the wood. There are two basic ways to deal with the problem: clean the crack out and round it over, which is a sensual way to enjoy the material rather than railing against its uncontrolled nature; or fill the crack with a mix of glue and wood dust. I prefer epoxy glue with color added to highlight the repair and emphasize the nature of the material.

I have had turnings dramatically blow apart while turning on the lathe. In a recent incident, I was able to save the fragments and glue them back together. This then became a feature of the bowl, titled Radiance, where the glue line was opened with a V-cut and then painted blue. To avoid this shattering experience, it is possible to strengthen the check before turning by inserting a glued wood dowel that becomes a feature of the design.

Play it up. Colored epoxy makes a feature of the check.

Radiance, 2008. Ash, paint. 16" (406mm) dia. x 17" (432mm).

Pegged Salad Bowl, 2012. Ash, paint. 17" (432mm) dia. x 8.5" (216mm).

Untitled Bowl 2012, now called Pegged Salad Bowl.

Wood in Motion

Learning to walk

In the work that led up to the walking bowls, I was looking for new expression through the cross section of turned forms, as well as for implied action and motion in their wooden-ness.

COLLECTION: PRIVATE, BRIGHT, ONTARIO.

Clam Shell, 1979. Soft maple, 11.5" (292mm) long.

Clam Shell continues to investigate the square shape first tried in the Egg Cup (page 78). The diagonal cuts were difficult and it took much flattening on a big sanding disk to get the shape. A sculptor purchased the piece; he was quick to understand the difficulty of making the shell form in wood.

Club Bowl, 1979. Australian walnut, 9.5" (241mm) long.

The club bowl was made soon after the Clam Shell using a similar diagonal cut, but the fit together was extremely difficult with this hard wood. The symmetry and stasis of the form, while enjoyed, was not pursued.

Mahogany Bowl, 1972. 10" (255mm) dia.

Opening the form forces consideration of the inside-outside relationships. Back and front becomes the new challenge.

Mahogany Bowl, 1972. 10" (255mm) dia.

This piece began as two bowl forms joined rim to rim; then I removed the wedge to allow access to the cross section and the inside.

Bowl, 1974. Western red cedar, 16" (406mm) dia.

The turning grooves went at right angles, making the piece difficult to mount on the lathe. If you turn too far you go through from one groove to the other. There is something comfortable, fluid, and sensual about this piece and I regret only making one.

Wooden Wood

The object speaks

Language played a part in how the walking bowl forms developed. People often refer to things made of wood as "wooden," and many objects I was seeing did look stiff, heavy, dumpy, poorly proportioned, and thoroughly wooden. I don't mean that something with strength, heft, guts, or boldness is not a relevant expression. But that is the question for both maker and viewer: What does the object express? How do we relate to it, what do we project onto it? For sure objects don't speak to me, but I do assign a quality to the object, and you may do the same. We may agree due to a common experience, but in the end it is the beholder who ultimately assigns the value to the object, however much the maker may complain.

COLLECTION: PRIVATE, TORONTO.

Walking Bowl, 1983. Zebrawood, 7" (178mm) x 8" (203mm) x 10" (254mm).

COLLECTION: PRIVATE, BUCKS COUNTY, PENNSYLVANIA.

Balancing Bowl, 1984. Red elm.

COLLECTION: PRIVATE, UTAH.

Subtle Expression. The walking bowl is an expressive form that can convey subtle gestures and feelings. The animated qualities of the walking bowls are essentially human and these pieces may also be made to run, stand, slope, balance, and perform most of the dancer's vocabulary.

Balancing Bowl, 1985. Zebrawood, 11" (279mm) high.

Right: Walking Bowl with Chainsaw Textures, 2012. Maple and paint, 10" (254mm) x 10" (254mm) x 8" (203mm). Collection: the artist.

CHAPTER 10

Faceplate turning, cut and rejoined

Batch of Boxes

Reassembled turnings decorate the lids

I have been collecting wooden boxes for many years but seldom make them. Maryann, my ex-wife, got me thinking about boxes in the early 1970s by sharing a couple she had collected. At the time I thought better boxes could be made. It's a good response for a maker and becomes like a challenge. Now there are about one hundred boxes in the collection, a few of mine and many collected during my trips to give workshops. The challenge to do better, whether better than one's own prior work or better than another, can drive the maker. Pushing yourself is best but I will occasionally indulge in a competitive response.

Most of the boxes I have made have been presents for family and friends. They have also sold well in galleries and shops. Recipe boxes to hold file cards are favorites, followed closely by jewelry boxes. The box itself is straightforward and standard woodworking, most of the design work is about the top where a turning, carving, or special piece of wood can be presented. The turning will often act as a handle to open things up. However this project is not so much about function as it is about the decorative potential of the fragmented turning.

When I make something I will often make two. If something goes wrong not all is lost, plus it is an opportunity to try a variation on the theme. One is a gift, the other will be sold. By the end of this project I had made four of various sizes, proportions, colors, and materials.

"This project is not so much about function as it is about the decorative potential of the fragmented turning."

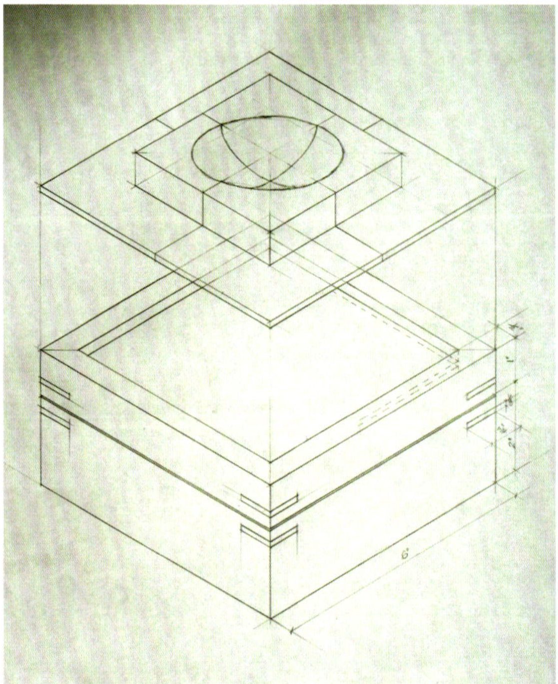

Basic Box. Simple box has mitered corner joints with reinforcing keys and a lid designed to display turned panels.

ALL PHOTOS BY MICHAEL MCLUHAN

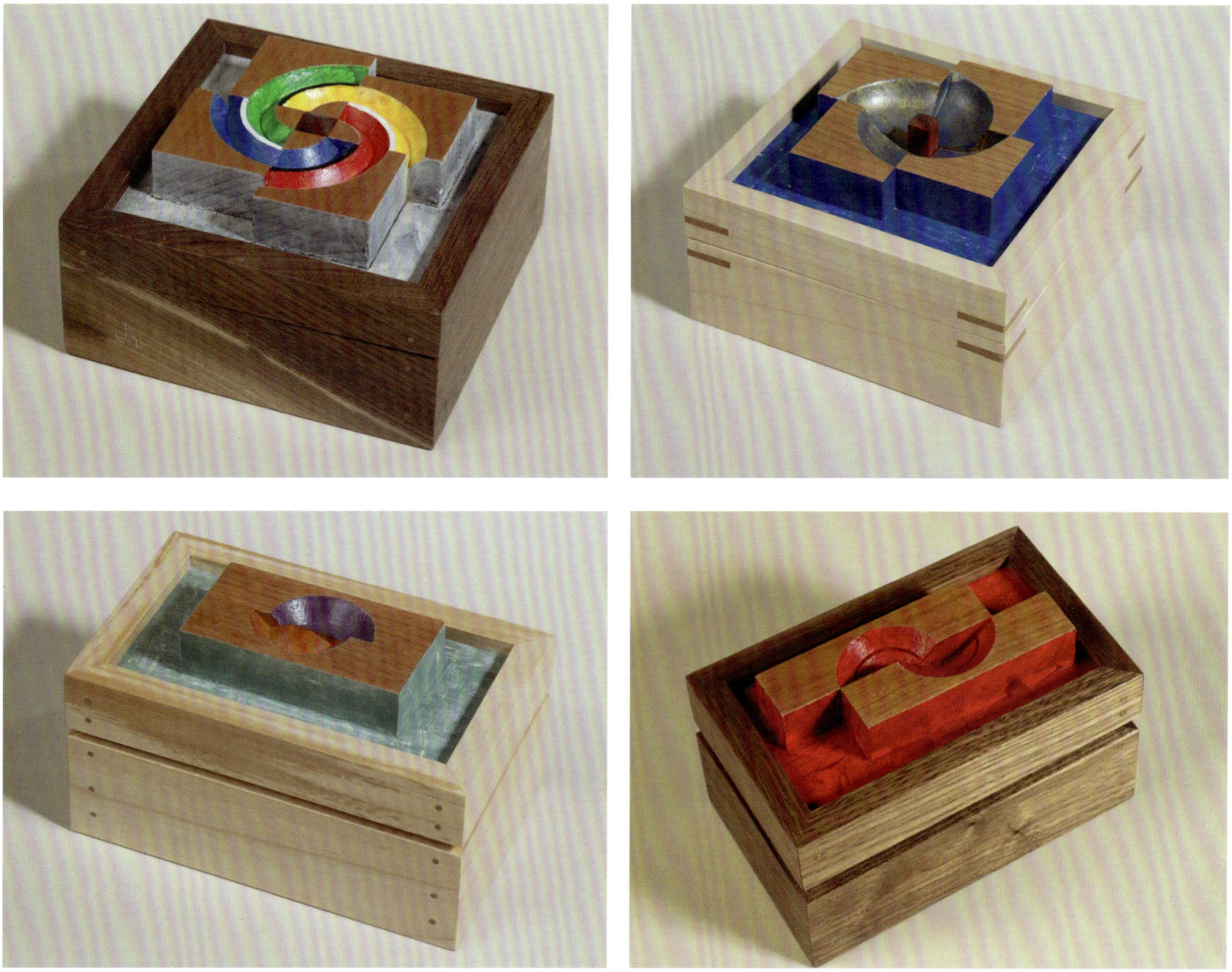

Four boxes, 2012. Various hardwoods, paint.

Choosing Colors

Selecting the color is always a pleasure, though it can be frustrating. These four boxes illustrate the questions and the process.

The box at top left looks at the color wheel. This color wheel is based on Johann Goethe, the German philosopher who theorized the primary colors as red, green, yellow, and blue. Later Johanne Itten eliminated green and just went with red, yellow and blue. So I go back and forth between these two schemas but rely mainly on Itten's work (see Paint and Color, page 40).

The box at bottom right is the safe way to go. The color of the wood is warm and dark in the red tones, the paint is a deep red. This relationship is called analogous colors. It's the easy way to go if you are not sure: decide what is the main color and choose a secondary color close to it on the color wheel. The towel rack (page 72) is a good example of analogous colors, orange red at the top, pure red in the middle, violet at the bottom.

The box at bottom left looks at complementary colors. They are opposite one another on the color wheel. They contrast one another. So the warm red tones of the wood get the opposite green.

The box at top right uses blue to contrast with the light yellow-brown wood, also a complementary color. In the hollow at the center the blue is washed over with translucent gold with a touch of red in it. It gives the blue depth and variety.

Prepare the materials

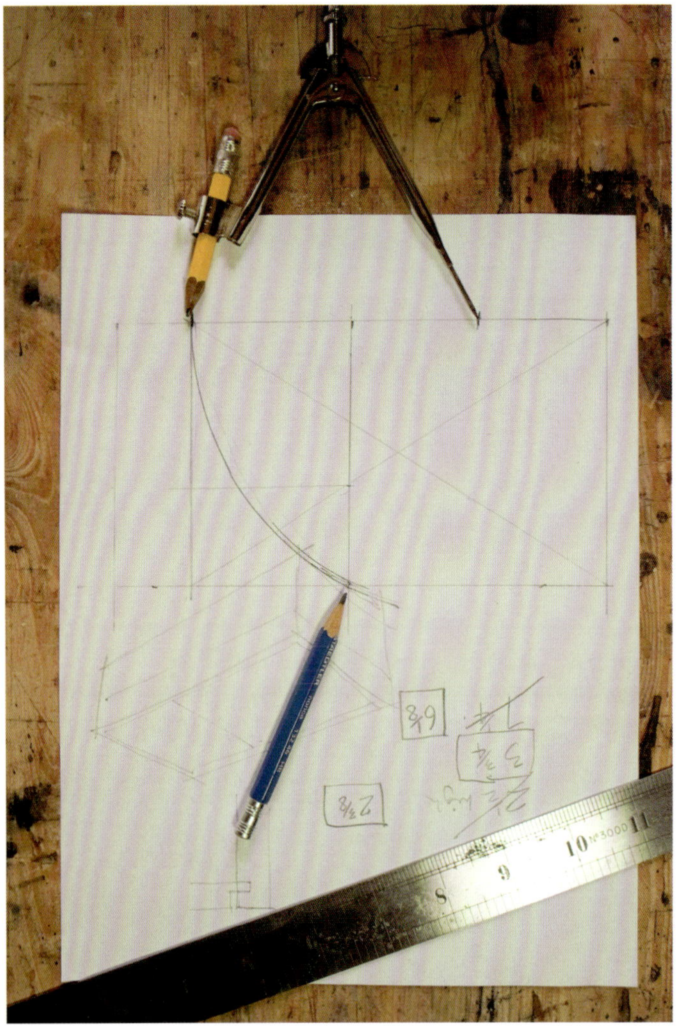

“Recipe boxes to hold file cards are favorites, as are jewelry boxes.”

1 **Proportions.** The design started with a discussion about jewelry boxes with my partner, Margaret, who brought out a leaded-glass box of the size that worked for her. I measured the box and then drew a rectangle using the Golden Section to establish a proportion I might like.

2 **Woods.** Assemble the materials: cherry for the tops, maple and walnut for the sides. Having marked the wood for the drawn rectangular proportions, I felt the box would look heavy compared to the original glass box so I made some pieces longer for square boxes.

3 **Sides and ends.** Cut the sides and ends to length on the table saw and miter them. Cut the first one to a marked-out dimension, then add a block to work as a stop.

4 **Grooves.** Mill grooves in the sides and ends to receive the bottom and top of the box.

5 **Test cuts.** When preparing the materials, cut an extra piece of each type for making test cuts. After sawing a batch of box sides and ends, I hold them together with elastic bands until all the pieces are ready for assembly.

6 **Dimensions.** With the box size established, it's possible to measure the groove and get the correct dimensions for the top and bottom panels. Machine the blanks to have wide flanges ⅛" (3mm) thick all around, to fit the table-sawn grooves in the box sides. Save the off-cuts for making cleats, in the next step.

Turn the lid

7 **Jigging.** The machined top needs a jig to hold it on the lathe. There are smart ways to do it with vacuum chucks, but this fixture is simple and quick. It's a plywood octagon with four cleats to retain the workpiece, and a faceplate screwed onto the other side.

8 **Accuracy.** Mark out and turn the design on the lathe. In this design there is not much turning, but it has to be accurate with dimensions that allow juxtaposition of the parts: the V-groove or cove being turned has to match the adjacent shape, so they'll connect when shifted.

Saw and Assemble

9 **Saw apart.** Take the turning out of the jig and saw it into four parts making sure the piece is cut through the center (see Design Investigations, page 120).

10 **Glue panel.** Gluing the four parts together is end-grain to end-grain, not great. I used extended-time PVA glue, pre-sized the end-grain with a coating of dilute glue, and then treated the glued-up piece gently until it was trapped by the box sides.

11 **Paint prep.** Use a good quality undercoat and paint just the areas where you want the color.

12 **Multiples.** While one panel is drying, glue and clamp up the next one. The advantage of making several at one time is revealed—the economy of multiples.

13 **Glue the box.** For the plywood bottom, squeeze a bead of glue into the groove on all four sides. This makes a good strong box. The solid-wood top will move with changing weather, so use only two dots of glue on opposite sides. Make sure to glue the ends of the panel and not the sides (see Wood Movement, page 120).

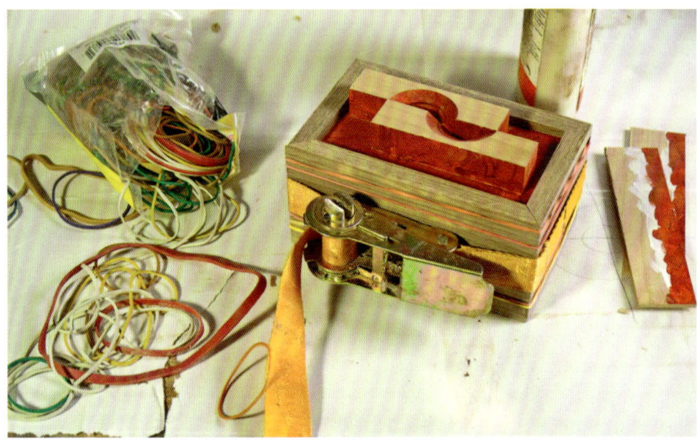

14 **Band clamp.** Hold the glued parts together with elastic bands. With good joints and lots of elastics, that might be enough if you don't have a band clamp. However, I use band clamps often and they are incredibly useful on any carcase work, even at this small scale.

15 **Clamp flat.** The paint really showed up every little inaccuracy, so for the second top I added a clamp to hold the four parts down flat, with a protective block that's waxed to resist glue.

Reinforce

16 **Strong corners.** Modern glues are impressive but the box needs a mechanical means to secure the corners. I take a simple and decorative approach, using splines or 3⁄16" (4.5mm) dowels as shown here. The layout also shows where I plan to saw the lid off the box.

17 **Jigging.** To make slots for decorative splines, a simple jig on the table saw makes a precise and parallel series of cuts.

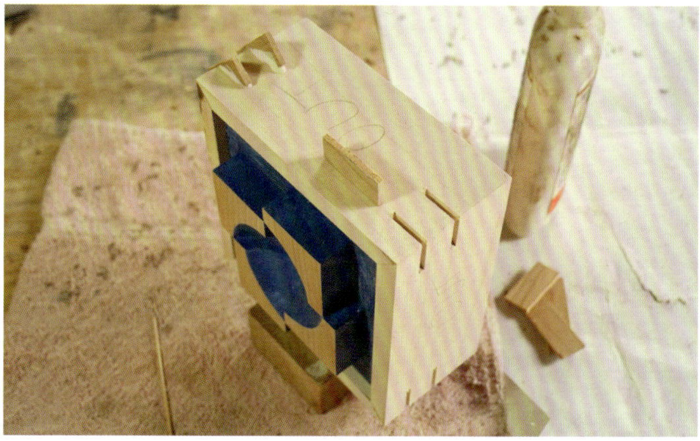

18 **Splines.** The off-cuts from the tops make good splines. The carpenter who framed my studio insisted on not cleaning up until the job was completed. It drove me crazy but I came to appreciate how useful it can be to find the right scrap of wood in the pile in the corner. Clean up after the project is complete.

"Take photos and make sketches to record the alternatives just in case they will become useful."

Open and line

19 Glue splines. Glue the splines into their slots, then saw and sand them flush after the glue has dried.

20 Saw lid. The lid gets cut off and then there is the big decision on how to bring the box back together. A wooden liner is the simplest solution and it can be detailed in more than one way.

21 Alignment. This liner has mitered ends and slots into the interior. The grain is not pronounced so the lid can be rotated and still sort of line up. Another box with striking diagonal figure would only go together in one way. But does the grain have to align? Well, not really, it just needs to look right.

22 Reveal. This liner creates a gap or reveal where the lid and bottom come together. The reveal may help to disguise an uneven connection, make a larger interior, or just look great by creating a shadow line articulating the form. It looks architectural, blocky, and constructed.

23 Varnish. The boxes are just about made but still need a final finish over the wood and color. They're small, so I will spray them with a can of satin-finish urethane varnish.

"Make more than one—if something goes wrong all is not lost."

Milling Machine

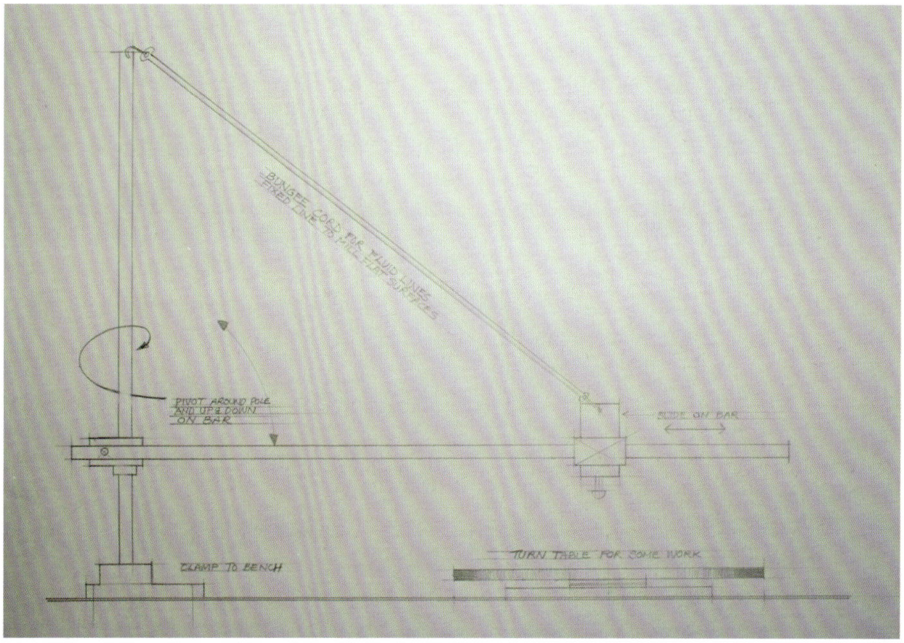

The milling machine consists of a router mounted on a pivoting arm, with a bungee mechanism that permits free up-down motion. Most of the parts were adapted from a Selecta Home Workshop device, a combination machine that included a drill press, which I inherited when moving from one workshop to another. One person's junk is another's treasure!

The post of the milling machine is 60" (520cm) tall by 1¾" (44mm) in diameter. There is a base that measures 16" (40cm) x 9" (23cm) with a steel socket into which I've inserted a wood dowel.

The machine has two arms of different lengths that can be combined. The short arm is 48" (120cm) and the longer is 60" (521cm) these may be joined to make 108" (644mm). The arms are pipes with an Inside diameter of 1⅜" (35mm) and outside diameter of 1⅝" (41mm) It is heavier than it needs to be, but it was convenient to make using materials that were available to me.

The router is mounted on a carriage that can travel along the arm. It may be secured by a thumbscrew at any point along the arm.

The arm is attached to the post using a simple block of hardwood drilled to fit over the post, with a bolt through the hardwood block attaching the arm. The arm will then rotate on two axes, vertical and horizontal.

The arm is controlled by a bungee cord that supports the weight of the router mounted on its carriage. For the short arm I use a 36" (91cm) bungee; the longer arm needs additional length. This arrangement gives finger-light control for delicate work. The arm may also be retained by a fixed rod, permitting surfaces to be milled flat. It's also possible to set up a template at the end of the arm, so a particular profile may be traced out.

The plywood work-supporting platform should be made to take whatever size you may want to mill; 20" (520cm) x 30" (76cm) has worked for most of my projects. It helps if the bottom plate is a bit larger than the workpiece, because it may need to be dragged around for some of the work.

It's also possible to place a turntable under the workpiece so that spirals and fluid shapes may be achieved. It is like rubbing your head and patting your stomach, but after some practice the dual motion becomes second nature and a highly versatile loose mark may be developed. Most woodworking uses a fence or a jig to control the line, but because it offers a fluid line this milling machine is quite atypical.

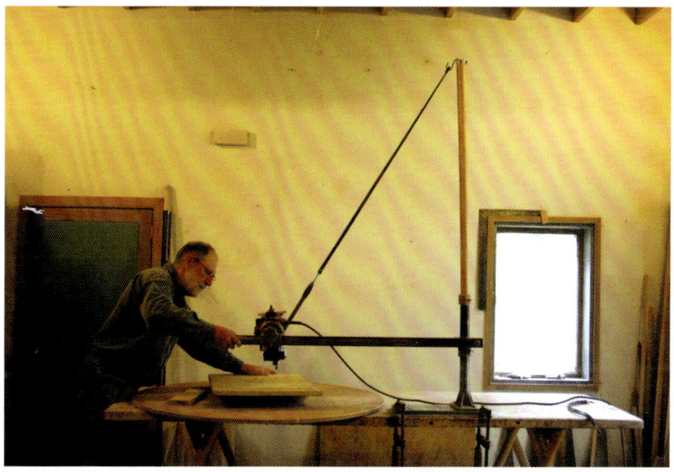

The sketch at top shows the principle behind the milling machine, shown in action in this photo and on page 118.

A scavenged mechanism mounts a router motor on the machine's pivoting arm.

The bungee arrangement permits easy up-down motion. The machine can follow a template or be used freehand.

Milled Surfaces

All the boxes are made the same way. The tops vary with either a carved design from the milling machine or a turned piece, just left as a turning or fragmented like the box in the picture. The milling machine unexpectedly develops a more organic patterning than turning, which is really caught in the geometry of the circle. The milling machine may also make circles and spirals but I really enjoy the ripples of sand and water. The bungee cord on the arm helps make a very fluid line that is surprisingly difficult to duplicate by regular carving methods. Depending on the wood and sharpness of the router bit, the surface may not need more than a light sanding to remove the wood hairs. Paint the color first and then do the milling. Conversely, carve the surface, slosh on the color, and then sand back to the flat plane leaving pools of color to contrast with the wood. Colored resin may also be used to fill the hollows and then sand back flat for the effect of an inlay. So many variations and combinations are possible.

Recipe Box, 1998. Maple, walnut, paint, 6.5" (165mm) x 7.5 " (191mm) square.

Recipe Box, 1998. Boxwood, padauk, 6" (152mm) x 7.25 " (184mm) square.

COLLECTION: PRIVATE, MAFRA, VICTORIA, AUSTRALIA.

Milling machine. After breaking free of the lathe to build the Toronto Library screen (pages 13 and 70), I made a smaller and more sophisticated machine for milling furniture-scale panels. It consists of a router mounted on a swivelling arm with a bungee mechanism that allows the operator to move the cutter fluidly into and out of the surface.

Collector's Cabinet

The cabinet takes the carving forward into larger pieces, which could also use fragmented turnings. The cabinet stand uses a connector like the ones discussed on page 138. The language keeps evolving, sometimes dramatically, but more often one step at a time.

Transitions

The entrance hall and corridor connected the kitchen, living room, dinning room, stairs, audio-visual room, and bedroom. The tiles were made by laminating a thick ash veneer onto Baltic birch plywood with a balancing veneer. They were ebonized with aniline dye, then cut to size with each one being different, and laid out in sections. The design to be carved was chalked onto the surface and then a group of tiles was laid out on the milling machine. My wonderful assistant at the time, Amanda Wal-Graff, kept careful notes and numbered the back of every tile. Like magic it all went down in the right order. The carpet was made off shore with the same shaped marks carrying the design up the stairs.

Opening Reception

The strips of wood were laid out on the milling machine and carved with regular arcs, then one was cut in half to make the panel that curves forward on the front of the reception desk, with its other half lying flat on the wall. I thought it was a very satisfactory articulation into the third dimension that embraced the idea of reception, but the prospective client said it was too much.

COLLECTION: PRIVATE, OWEN SOUND, ONTARIO.

Collector's Cabinet, 2004. Cherry, holly, maple, 50.5" (280mm) x 15.5" (394mm) square.

Opening Reception, maquette, 2011. Wood ebonized and carved.

COLLECTION, PRIVATE, OWEN SOUND, ONTARIO.

Connections and Transitions, 2005. Ash veneer on plywood, ebonized and carpeted; 30' x 14' on one level and up the stairs.

Design Investigations

You may be reading this book for project ideas and shop techniques, but for me it is as much about demonstrating design methods and staying open to new ideas, even accidental ones.

When making tops for the boxes shown on page 111, I mistakenly cut the first one off center and had to make another with the extra blank cut at the start (Step 5). Then I took a break from box-making to look at some different ways of putting the pieces back together.

This is a good mental exercise in creative thinking. Usually I will try a few variations, never more than about twenty. Suspend judgment until you run out of ideas, have fun and see what happens. It is low risk and it cannot be wrong because there is no criteria to measure against. The photos are a bit rough because they weren't taken for publication, but rather, they are sketches of how I saw these pieces during the process. For me the sketch will often carry an energy and excitement not found in a finished work.

Even after the creative exercising I go back to the original idea conceptualized for the box. I don't have to stay with it, but it's too easy to get sidetracked. So I take photos and make sketches, to record the alternatives just in case they will become useful. Making a record is really important because the next day I can never remember all the variations. The startling insight will vanish and reconstructing it may not reveal the "Aha!" moment.

If you have doubts about your creative ability, try a simple exercise. Give it a few minutes each morning for a week, just like the White Queen in Lewis Carroll's *Through the Looking Glass:* "Why, sometimes I've believed as many as six impossible things before breakfast." Start out by asking, "How many ways can I use a...." Try it with the following objects and take two minutes to write down every idea.

How many ways can I use a pencil?

—6" duct tape?

—paper clip?

—magnifying glass?

—computer CD?

—cardboard shoe box?

—hammer?

The first week may be tough, but if you keep going and go through the list again the following week, the creative muscles will be getting exercised and soon you will be a whole lot better at it. It takes time to make automatic an expansive and exploratory response. Objects are what we make, but this process may be applied in many other ways too.

Wood Movement

Wood movement is always an issue, not only in general woodworking but also in turning. It's why green-wood turnings dry oval, and why the solid-wood panel that forms the box lid needs to be trapped in grooves that allow for some movement. Solid wood changes its dimensions not only as a result of drying after being cut from the tree, but also in response to weather. Finishes can slow wood movement down, but won't prevent it.

It's not always easy to anticipate wood movement when turnings are involved, but if you look at the end grain you can figure out what to expect.

Plywood vs. solid. Glue the plywood into its groove to make the box strong, but use just a dot for the solid-wood panel so it can move.

CHAPTER 11

Spindle turnings, quartered for legs and rails

Steeple Table

Turnings reclaim old church spire

The spire for St. George's church had to be replaced, a huge expense for a lively congregation that was up to the task. Over the years many letters have been written in the local newspaper about historical buildings and the importance of keeping this material culture as evidence of lives well lived. Lighting a fire one day I saw the article about the spire in the newspaper and then scrunched it up and threw it in the firebox of the wood stove. After a moment I pulled it out and kept the article; then I heard there might be an auction for raising funds. Months later artists from the region were offered the materials from dismantling the old steeple because the fire marshal wanted all the stuff cleared from the church basement. A few of us turned up and raked through a full basement of this old dirty lumber and sheets of roofing metal. Michael McLuhan, the photographer for this book, joined me as I pulled some larger pieces of wood. The day developed a nice camaraderie between the organizers and the artists. Later I went back, after the lead organizer called to say that some larger sections of wood had been found and set aside.

Small objects for the auction were an obvious choice, but I also wanted to make a larger and more significant piece using the vocabulary I had developed over the years. Some very short lengths of wood seemed insignificant and probable firewood. The pieces of the old steeple did not release an idea until I looked at a large piece for table legs and then the short lengths were clearly right for the tabletop. Rather than clean the wood I decided to keep the aged church dirt and contrast it with the pristine old-growth wood inside.

The design of the table was to reflect the steeple in its tall proportions. The tabletop plan became an eight-sided figure, the same as the footprint of the old steeple. The wood was thick enough to make a substantial top and get a strong joint with the legs. I have made similar tables and stools using a single turning to make four legs (see page 130), though in the past I always placed the right-angle of the legs in cross section on the inside. This time the turned part is on the inside. The protruding nails, which seemed to be part of the material's ethos, were too vicious to expose.

The table did well at auction where one of the other regional artists, Joan Hawksbridge, purchased the piece during a rousing evening when the artists and the congregation were able to celebrate saving the steeple and rebuilding a major landmark in the beautiful historic city of Owen Sound.

"Then the commission becomes a symbiotic collaboration and a wonderfully rich human exchange."

COLLECTION: JOAN HAWKSBRIDGE, OWEN SOUND, ONTARIO. PHOTO: MICHAEL MCLUHAN.

Steeple Table, 2012. Salvaged wood, paint, 34" (864mm) tall.

Reclaiming old wood

THE SUN TIMES

OWEN SOUND: Renovating St. George's Anglican Church stone tower and spire has blossomed into $360,000 project

WILLY WATERTON The Sun Times

Brian McClelland, with Roof Tile Management of Mississauga, is the supervisor of the St. George's steeple restoration job.

WILLY WATERTON The Sun Times

St. George's Anglican Church steeple is undergoing major renovations. The cost has grown from $150,000 to $360,000.

Architectural 'gem' well worth saving, church members say

PAUL JANKOWSKI
Sun Times staff

There's an almost palpable sense of pride among those at St. George's Anglican Church most closely involved in the restoration work that's going on there.

What began in 2006 as a warning in an engineer's report that the stone tower that holds up the soaring spire had to be repaired or torn down — something they thought would cost them $150,000 — has grown into a more than $360,000 project to restore both those parts of the church so they may last for another 100 years or more.

There are fewer than 200 people in St. George's congregation now and "nobody really wealthy. We don't have any wealthy parishioners," Nancy King, who chairs the fundraising committee for the project, said in an interview. "It's just a huge, huge thing for us to undertake."

"We've tried everywhere we could think of to get any kind of financial support from any branch of government and there's just no money for churches."

The congregation voted unanimously to proceed with the project anyway.

St. George's is one of the four stone churches at 10 St. E. and 4th Ave. E., a collection that gave the intersection the nickname Salvation Corners. When it was opened and dedicated on Aug. 7, 1881, a church pamphlet says, "It was considered (and still is) one of the most beautiful churches in Ontario."

Built at a cost of $12,000, "St. George's Church is constructed of stone ashlar in the Gothic style. The steeple measures 142 feet in height and that measurement is directly proportional to all of the measurements in the church — the nave and chancel are exactly the same length and the distance between the north and south transepts is exactly half that distance," the pamphlet says.

The church was designed by Marshall Aylesworth, the architect behind some dozen churches and 24 other buildings, according to Laurie McBride, a masters of art history student at York University who is researching his work. She calls St. George's "the most spectacular" of the Anglican churches he designed.

See STEEPLE, Page A8

OWEN SOUND: Sixteen camps across Ontario to be sold

1 **Old news.** Newspaper saved from the wood stove tells about the steeple reclamation project.

"I decided to keep the aged church dirt and contrast it with the pristine old-growth wood inside."

2 **Old materials.** Here is the salvaged material and now come the design choices: how to find the steeple again?

3 **Tabletop.** Join the short boards for the tabletop with biscuits and waterproof PVA glue. If this table becomes a plant stand it may well have water spilled on the surface.

4 **Glue and clamp.** Clamp the boards for the tabletop together so the glue can dry.

5 **Many nails.** The plank for the legs contained rather a lot of nails so it had to be cut apart with a hack saw when the band saw reached each nail.

Turning the legs

6 **Spindle bundle.** A hose clamp bundles the four legs for turning. The bevel sawn off the corners facilitates the hose clamp. A small amount of glue applied to the inside ends of the bundled pieces stops the wood from slipping in the hose clamp if or when the chisel catches.

7 **Hose clamp.** On a long length like this I would also place a hose clamp in the middle. Slim strips tend to yawn apart on the lathe and as the turning gets smaller they really open up. As a result the edges of the wood may splinter.

8 **Save the nails.** Locating and marking the nails will save the edge of the turning tool. Pare back with a mallet and chisel, working up to the nail. These old nails were so firmly rusted it was better not to remove them. Nails are essential to the story, symbolic in various ways for the church.

9 **Shoulder.** Turn a shoulder at the tabletop end of the legs but leave it in the rough-turned state, because sanding invariably knocks the circle into an oval.

10 **Unbundle.** Separate the four legs by removing the band clamp and then tapping with the chisel on the glue line.

Joining the table

11 **Saw joint.** Band-saw the tabletop into an eight-sided figure and then saw a half-moon from four of the facets to receive the legs. Smooth the curved plane on a belt-sander drum.

12 **Cross rail.** The cross rail can be seen in the glue up at the bottom of the table. Cut a single turning in half down its length and then rotate the two halves through 90 degrees to form the cross.

13 **Color.** I painted the sphere of the cross rail the same green as the leg at the tabletop.

14 **Dowels.** The glue would have been enough to hold the leg to the tabletop, but to be sure I added the mechanical fixing of a dowel. I left the ends of the dowels proud and painted them green.

15 **Jigging.** Strap the vee-block to the leg with masking tape and then clamp it, to guide the bit and prevent breakout while drilling for the dowels. For maximum accuracy the vee-block was pre-drilled in the drill press.

Final touches

16 **Adding words.** The table lacked something and I put it away away for a couple of weeks. The green paint on top of the leg called for too much attention. With the green removed the facets on the edge needed something and after some deliberation I painted, on the sides of the tabletop, the word H-O-P-E.

17 **Looks good.** The table works well as a plant stand.

Subject and Object

Subjects are often difficult; the subject may reveal or open our thinking toward the human condition, but it is as likely to mystify or confront expectations. A quality of art is the jolt to think more deeply about something, so the object that carries ideas will often get left behind. The viewer then becomes the editor and perhaps thinks about the overt function or construction of the object, or perhaps about the subject raised by the title, image, or the maker's choice of colors. Take your pick or pick all—that's the maker's lot, to think through all of it.

Stratum, 1973. Walnut, 13" high (330mm).

Faces emerge

The walnut bowl is stood on end and the family of faces emerges as a series of profiles (top photo). The fact that it's a woodturning quickly gives way to the implications of one face to another. While they do not have a specific meaning, most people will ponder the faces as representing child and adult profiles. What is their relationship? The turning technique carries the idea or subject forward. The subject, the faces, becomes progressively dominant as one looks at the piece.

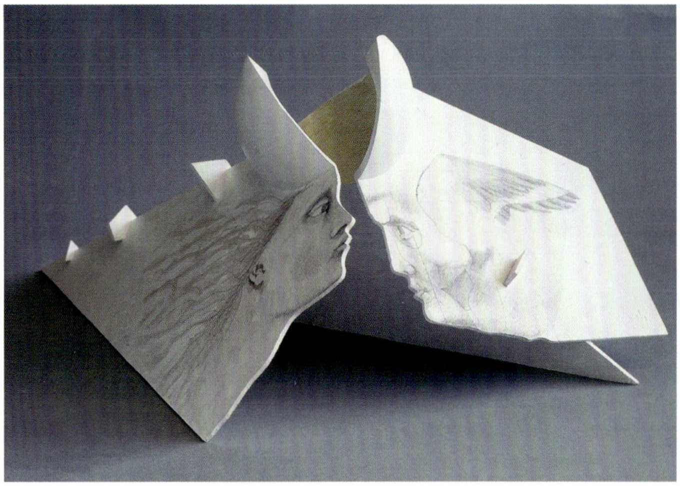

Psyche and Mercury, 1990. Wood, paint, graphite, 10" (254mm) x 23" (584mm) x 16" (406mm).

Two faces

A man and a woman, who might they be? This is where the title, Psyche and Mercury, introduces the viewer to the idea of Greek myths. But Psyche, the god of love, and Mercury, now identified as the god of commerce, never met in the ancient myths. So what might they be talking about? The object-ness gets pretty much lost with minimal turning and flat surfaces, but the arrangement does suggest a dialog. The viewer is left to think about the exchange between Psyche and Mercury.

Symmetry

The face profiles surrounding the wall mirror, bottom, are recognizably from the same turning, perhaps that's why they do not carry the same interest as the faces in (the other two pieces shown here). Consequently the viewer is more likely to think about how it was made or why made in that particular configuration. Surrounding a mirror may enliven the contents of the mirror, which in this photo merely reflects the rest of the exhibition. While the piece seems to have potential, it does not appear to extend a subject very far.

Wall Mirror, 1975. Southern sassafras, 16.5" (419mm) x 6" (152mm) square.

Subject and Object in Context

We all live in a context that in part we make, and that in part is handed to us. We choose the subject, we make the object, and we place it in the context. The object we have made is full of ourselves and we may become the subject. Listening to the music is one thing, and it will change according to where we are and who we are with. Sometimes we are only interested in listening to the music, while at other times we will be interested in the score, the composer, the context in which it was created, where it is being played, and who we are with. Everything is a woven fabric that connects together the threads of our lives, objects help carry the story along.

Memories

The way we see objects and subjects and the way we think about them is complex. It would be nice to keep it simple but then the subtlety often gets lost. This piece with the two needles is as much about the object and perception of it as it is about a subject. The two needles are exactly the same size and yet because of their different contexts—one on the mirror and the other on a carved surface—they appear to be different sizes. The subject of needles is not really addressed in this piece. However, it would be possible, even delightful, for the viewer to make up something about the pair of needles, their relationship, and their significance.

Illusion

Thread for Needle looks at illusion. The needle is real or almost, since it is made of wood and painted silver to look like the real thing. It is really a large model of a needle. The thread, etched out of the silver backing, hangs in the mirror also suggesting the real thing. When the object is not real it alludes to a subject, in this case the subject of sewing. The viewer and indeed the maker will inevitably think about sewing things together as they see their own reflections. Mirrors are usually associated with narcissism, but the subject here is first of all still about the needle and the thread.

Thread for Needle, 1999. Wood, paint, mirror. Collection: Private, Trarelgon, Australia

Provocation

The hat looks like a thimble. The thimble protects the finger on the hand. The similar shapes create a relationship between head and hand. Really one hat would be enough but through the use of mirrors, four hats emerge. I have spent many years tracking and creating four-element quadrilateral relationships as an antidote to simplistic dualities. A typical quad might be self, subject, object, context, the four things I think about when making anything. They are my four thinking hats that also protect and enable my hands.

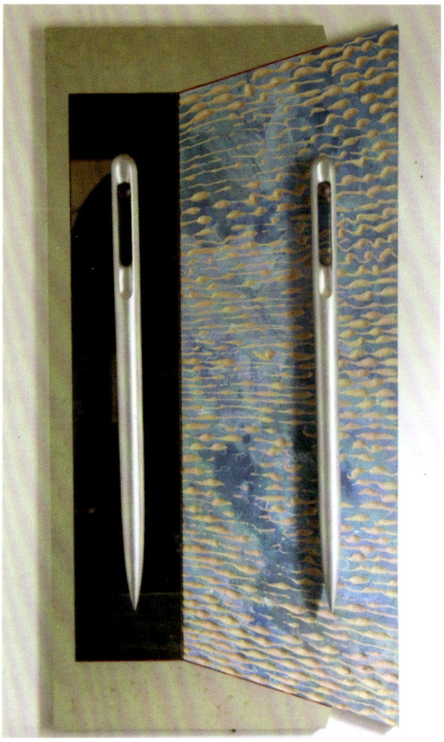

Memories of Unthreaded Needles, 1998. Wood, mirror, paint, 44.5" (1130mm) x 23" (584mm) x 2" (51mm). Collection: the artist.

Four Hats, 1999. Wood, paint, mirror; 19" (483mm) x 14" (356mm) x 8" (203mm). Collection: Private, Victoria, Australia.

CHAPTER 12

Spindle turning, cut and joined

Stool Collaboration

Conic connector supports layers of meaning

Stools, like tables, need strong joints. The conic connector answers that need, though it is laborious to make and not a solution for production. It is a craft design, unless thousands were to be made—the tooling would be simple.

This stool was not a client project, but rather, a collaboration over a set of parts brought out of storage to complete the brief for this book: if you're going to experiment with fragmented woodturnings, you'll need serviceable furniture joints. Artistic collaborations are common in the woodturning field though here, my collaborator was John Kelsey, the book's editor and a man of words. We two have worked together before, notably on essays for *Fine Woodworking* magazine and on my second book, *Appearance and Reality: A Visual Handbook for Artists, Designers and Makers* (Cambium Press, 2000).

Working with a collaborator offers an interesting comparison to working with a client. The client or his environment often edits the maker's idea and finding the interesting compromise becomes the challenge. In a collaboration, each player takes his turn and puts his own mark on the piece. I designed and made the stool; its joinery makes the object interesting enough to stand on its own. John wrote words on it, adding a subject to the object and another layer of meaning too. At the moment the context for the stool is this book and the exhibition that will accompany its publication, but after that, who knows?

"The commission becomes a symbiotic collaboration and a wonderfully rich human exchange."

Stool: The Hot Seat, Stephen Hogbin with John Kelsey, 2012. Maple, paint, black pen, 26" tall.

Conic connection

1 **Parts.** The stool parts include quarter-turned legs, slab seat, and conic connectors. Starting from an earlier stool shown on page 135, the legs move from the center of the seat to the outside. The base becomes a set of four rails split from turnings. The quarter-turned legs are too slender for a stool; the conic connector solves that.

2 **Turning.** To make the conic connector cut 1 ¼" (32mm) squares of hardwood and saw a rebate along one edge. Glue the off-cut back into the rebate, just a dab of glue at both ends, to help mount it on the lathe so you can turn the shape, conic or whatever. Remove from the lathe and knock out the glued-in wedge.

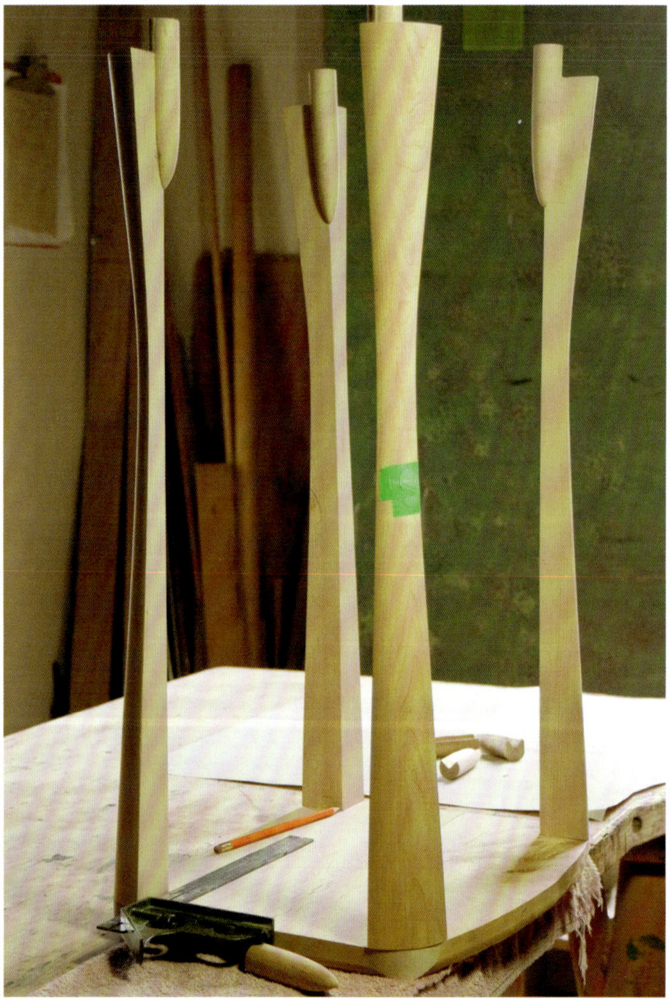

3 **Layout.** Stand the legs upside-down on the seat to mark out where to drill for the conic's tenon. Fit the legs and measure for the rail lengths.

4 **Spacer.** Also at this point make a spacer for the legs, a plate of notched plywood shown in Step 6, to assist in the complex glue-up to come.

Dowel the rails

5 **Wood.** Turn the rails from 1 x 2" (25 x 51mm) lengths of maple. Finish the inside surfaces first and then with a tiny amount of glue on both ends clamp them together with hose clamps for turning. The rails are different lengths; they can be from two turnings or cut from one long one.

6 **Dowels.** Locate the dowels that will join the rails to the legs. This leg orientation permits the square ends of the rails to butt against the flat surfaces of the legs.

7 **Drill rails.** Jig the rails on the drill press table so you can be sure to drill straight and square holes for the joining dowels. Here I've rotated the table to the vertical so I can clamp the rails to it.

8 **Drill legs.** Clamp and drill the dowel holes in the legs. Note that each leg receives two holes drilled into its adjacent flat faces; the holes should meet.

9 **Fit dowels.** Cut one end of each dowel at 45 degrees so they can meet inside the drilled holes. Fit and glue ⅜" or ½" dowels before test-assembling the stool. Label all parts with up/down, right/left—it is easy to get something backward.

Assembly

10 **Glue.** Clamp gently but make sure there is a tiny bead of squeezed-out glue encircling each joint. Leave until the glue is leather hard and then remove the squeeze-out, but keep the clamps on overnight. I use extended-open PVA glue to give me time to work at a comfortable pace.

11 **Bracing.** The ball shapes glued inside the rails reinforce the dowel joint and help brace the structure. They have flat surfaces for gluing, made on the disk sander. You could add a screw but here the glue is enough.

12 **Visual echo.** The ball shapes, painted orange, visually repeat the conics under the seat.

Collaborations with Clients

The first stool using the conic joint detail was made in 2006 for a client (photo at right). Their telephone table needed a stool in the kitchen. I had been thinking about an architectural expression of post and beams, how to express structure and the forces involved, how to construct strong tables and chairs using slender fragments of long spindles.

This stool, like the table for the church steeple auction (page 122), also is about working with other people. More than half of my production is with clients. They ask me if I will make something and then we talk. The discussion is about working with them rather than working for them: I am not in a service industry and if the rapport is poor I will suggest someone else. Fortunately, most of my clients will say, "We like your ideas, have seen your work, and would like to live with something you have made." Then the commission becomes a symbiotic collaboration and a wonderfully rich human exchange. However, it still has to work for them and that's what makes it symbiotic. For the 2006 kitchen stool I made a plate-type base to show off the conic connection. No chance of missing it with the upside/downside configuration, and fortunately the client was delighted.

First connection. The conic connector first appeared on this kitchen stool made for a client in 2006. It allows slender quarter-turnings to make a strong architectural joint.

Strong connection. With the mechanics worked out, the conic connector evolved to become a strong decorative element in many furniture projects, such as this stool and others shown on the next two pages.

Tables and Stools

There are a number of table designs where the leg connects to the frame of the table. One turning makes four legs and this detail works extremely well. While glue would be quite sufficient on a small table, I still put a screw through from the back. With the table turned upside down, a triangular block is on the inside of the rails and a single screw is passed through the triangular block and into the leg (below right).

The solution is similar for the two-faceted leg, which makes a stronger structure for larger tables. The foot for this design uses the conic connector (page 132) and note again the surfaces do not run flush between the leg and the foot. (bottom right)

Some of the connections become quite decorative while still adding structurally to the joint. The stool rails are made from a single turning and then the problem of cutting a triangular hole for the rail is resolved with the addition of the shaped connector.

Even without a lathe its possible to give a turned look to the leg using a router. It is quicker and easier to use a router sometimes (lower left, facing page).

Georgian Bluffs Table, 2008. Maple, paint. 23" (584mm) x 23.5" (597mm) square.

COLLECTION: THE ARTIST.

Cooking up a Stool, 2008. Maple, paint. 28" (710mm) x 15" (381mm) square.

The foot becomes quite decorative.

Leg connects to table frame.

Two-part leg has shaped filler block.

Foot repeats conic detail.

Pearwood Table, 2004.
Ash, pearwood, walnut, paint; 30" (760mm) x 16" (406mm) square.

Routed details resemble turnings.

Ebonized Table. 2004. Ash, aniline dye, paint. 24" (610mm) x 22" (559mm) square.

Chair Connectors

Furniture, like architecture, is all about connections, transitions, and relationships among parts. Recently I made an armchair that articulated the connection with an unusual joint. Bringing the parts together to make a featureless sphere is possible, but wood moves, and with any change in moisture the joint shows a hairline crack or worse. Making the distinctions clear is better, and I was taught as a student to not make flush surfaces because they never stay the same.

COLLECTION: MARGARET BALLANTYNE, ONTARIO, CANADA. PHOTO: MICHAEL MCLUHAN.

Her Chair, 2011. Ash, upholstery; 38" (985mm) x 25" (635mm) x 22" (559mm).

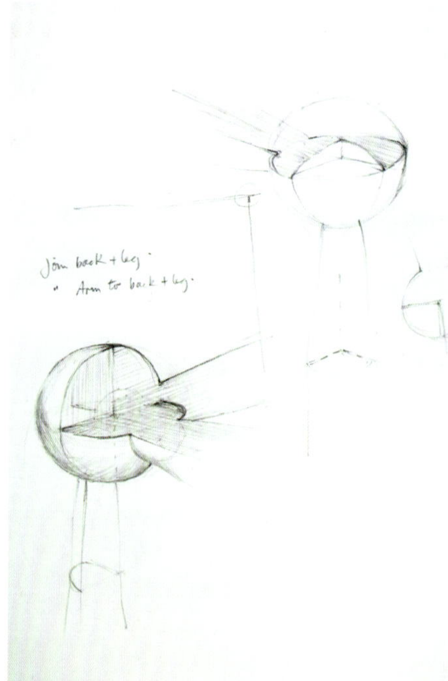

Three-way ball joint for chairs.

PHOTO: MICHAEL MCLUHAN.

Small ball is glued in last.

Decorative finish at the front.

Table Connection

The glass top of the table has the word "connection" sandblasted into the surface. Actually the word repeats itself in almost a mirror image, connected by the last letter of each word. Looking through the table we see many different turned elements making up a structure of connections. Looking at the words the viewer may well think about different connections besides wood joints made with turned parts. The juxtaposition of the words is about the subject of relationships.

The concept for this piece was first developed as a commission for a family in Ottawa. The table was to stand between two chairs, connecting them in the room. During my previous visit to Ottawa, I spent time walking along the river and the Rideau Canal, and the boat-like form was inspired in part by those walks.

COLLECTION: PRIVATE, TARA, ON, CANADA

Connections, 2005. Ash, paint, glass; 27" (686mm) x 34" (863mm) x 19" (483mm).

Subject and Object: A Meditation on Decay

These concrete slabs, cast from a large faceplate turning not unlike the trivet disk in Chapter 6, have been with me a long time and seem to get heavier each time I move them. They were an exploration of materials and of how the different materials would interact with the environment. The original pattern was turned in closed-cell Styrofoam, then cast in plaster to make a mold for the concrete pours.

I take a slow pleasure in watching the cast concrete pieces respond to the seasons and the environment, as they slowly sink into the ground. I don't think I will be moving them again.

Ripples

The first piece was a single circle of ripples. It gathered water and reflected the sky and its surroundings. I was interested in how the environment would interact with the object. Over time the deepest pools turned red with algae and the shallow ones turned green from a different algae. I thought that was a satisfying discovery.

Circles

The next piece was a four-part set of circles. When casting the concrete I treated each surface differently, by adding materials that included egg shells, wood prunings, soot from the fireplace, and broken shards of stone. I was interested how each surface would interact with the environment. There is something intriguing about old ruins, worn surfaces from use, and decay when it is outside oneself. The pieces were cast in 1989 and since then their surfaces have deteriorated surprisingly little. There is still some egg shell, and the stone shards have remained attached. The soot has worn away as have most of the sticks, leaving the hollows where they were.

Circles.

Ripples.

Getting older

A couple of years ago the Buddha turned up and sits in contemplation of the changing nature of materials, an interesting subject to contemplate as I get older. The object and the subject are mutually supportive as the castings age. The gentle snow covering keeps the ideas warm until spring.

Apple petals

I really like the petal covering from the apple tree. It has a gentleness and is a welcome sight each spring. Catching the moment when the pattern was at its best required an almost daily visit. The seasons move around and the subject transforms the object.

Getting older.

Apple petals.

Index